FINANCIAL SYSTEM, FINANCIAL DEVELOPMENT AND FIRM SURVIVAL

Adnan KARA / Ramazan SAYAR (eds.)

FINANCIAL SYSTEM, FINANCIAL DEVELOPMENT AND FIRM SURVIVAL

PERSPECTIVES FROM TURKISH FINANCIAL SYSTEM AND GLOBALIZATION

PETER LANG

Bibliographic Information published by the Deutsche Nationalbibliothek
The Deutsche Nationalbibliothek lists this publication in the Deutsche Nationalbibliografie; detailed bibliographic data is available online at http://dnb.d-nb.de.

Library of Congress Cataloging-in-Publication Data
A CIP catalog record for this book has been applied for at the Library of Congress.

Printed by CPI books GmbH, Leck

ISBN 978-3-631-80631-9 (Print)
E-ISBN 978-3-631-81463-5 (E-PDF)
E-ISBN 978-3-631-81464-2 (EPUB)
E-ISBN 978-3-631-81465-9 (MOBI)
DOI 10.3726/b16834

Peter Lang – Berlin · Bern · Bruxelles · New York · Oxford · Warszawa · Wien

This publication has been peer reviewed.

www.peterlang.com

Foreword

Trade is a phenomenon that occurs when people buy and sell. More and more people are affected by trade. As the product variety and durability increases, so does the trade. In addition, strengthening the trust of people in the market and becoming the seller of consumers in the market is expanding the scope of trade. On the international scale, trade is no longer limited to what developed countries do, but developing countries are also involved in global exchange. Developing countries that act as new players in global trade establish new trade blocks by signing agreements with countries with which they have close relations in order to integrate faster. These developments, which have caused political turmoil in global trade, have brought about the redesign of monetary and financial systems. The alternatives of New York and London, which have an important position in the world financial system, are being evaluated. Some of the developments in the financial system in recent years are as follows; The European Union's use of the Euro as its currency, the financial cooperation between China and Russia in Shanghai, the use of a common currency in African countries, the emergence of blockchain as digital currencies. The main aim of the book is to examine the development of the country's financial system on survival of the firm. Chapter one examines the relationship between marketing finance, infrastructure and entrepreneurship. Chapter two examines literature review study which consists of theoretical framework of the relationship between export and export financing. Chapter three examines the interactive effects of remittances and financial development on Turkey's economic growth. In Chapter four, big three credit rating agencies and sovereign credit ratings determined by these institutions are emphasized. Chapter five examines the concept of financialization and the relationship between income inequality. Chapter six examines the pricing system in national and global markets.

Contents

Contributors

Adnan Kara

Bayburt University, Economics and Administrative Sciences Faculty, Bayburt, Turkey

Bülent Günsoy

Anadolu University, Economics Faculty, Eskişehir, Turkey

Derya Yalçin

Nişantaşı University, Vocational High School, Logistics Programme, İstanbul, Turkey

Yılmaz Onur Ari

Bayburt University, Economics and Administrative Sciences Faculty, Bayburt, Turkey

Özgür Bayram Soylu

Kocaeli University, Economics and Administrative Sciences Faculty, Kocaeli, Turkey

Ramazan Sayar

Bayburt University, Economics and Administrative Sciences Faculty, Bayburt, Turkey

Ümit Yıldız

Bayburt University, Economics and Administrative Sciences Faculty, Bayburt, Turkey

About the Authors...

Lynn Schaal is an author, musician, motivational speaker, and founding pastor of Amazing Grace Fellowship in Twin Falls, ID. Lynn's passion is to equip and empower people with knowledge that can bring positive change on a practical level. Lynn has traveled extensively around the world helping people reach their God-given potential. Lynn and his wife, Dorette, have five children.

Gus Brackett is president and founder of Two Fishes Investment, LLC. He graduated from Utah State University in 1998 and earned a Masters in Business Administration from Northwest Nazarene University in 2001. Gus currently resides with his wife and four children on a cattle ranch in southwest Idaho.

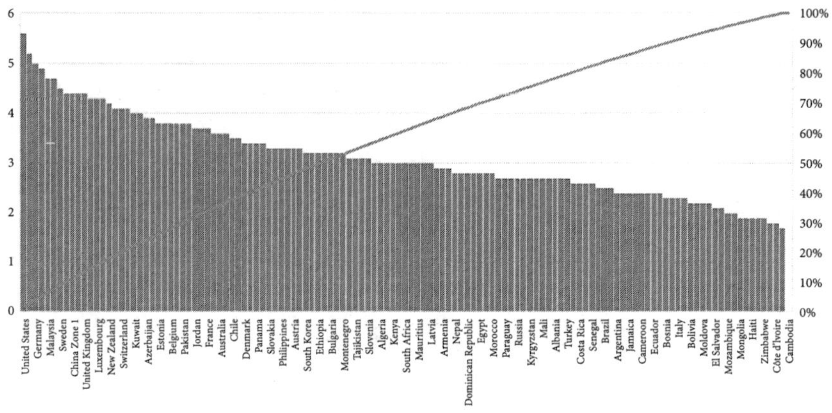

Fig. 2: Venture Capital According to Countries. Source: Created Based on WEF Competitiveness Index Data

the increase in efficiency of the project-based technologic initiatives. In addition to providing funds for venture capital, it also provides consultancy support from the investor in strategy, finance, marketing, and management (Fig. 2).

It can be said that marketing has a key role in providing competitive environment which is important for consumers. The task of marketing is to determine the needs and desires of the market and to effectively fulfill them. The task of production is to efficiently convert inputs into outputs in line with marketing decisions. Basically, without production capabilities, marketing cannot fulfill its duties. One of the major inputs of production is capital. In this respect, economies with advanced financial system are superior in terms of high-scale production capabilities. According to a study conducted with panel data of 65 countries for 30 years, the proportion of goods produced in the Domestic National Product is high in the countries with advanced financial system; and produced goods constitute a high proportion of total exports (Beck, 2002). Economies with advanced financial system are also successful in marketing due to their high production capabilities. The best examples of these are that countries such as Japan and China first succeed in production productivity and technological development, and then release their global brands.

An undeveloped financial system presents many problems for enterprises. Especially financial crises are a big obstacle for marketing. Developments in financial markets are also hampered by crises. Financial crisis arises as a result of the sudden depreciation of a large part of the financial services institutions or

assets. Financial crisis, a subspecies of economic crises, has many causes. Some reasons are speculative attacks, weaknesses in financial structure, deterioration in the structure of the economy, increase in interest rates, excessive fluctuations in capital movements, global financial situation, deterioration of financial sector balance sheets and increased uncertainties (anapara.com, 25.06.2019). According to the surveys conducted with managers within the scope of the global competitiveness index survey prepared by the World Economic Forum (WEF), access to finance is one of the biggest obstacles in doing business in most economically underdeveloped countries. Due to the cash shortage experienced during crises that restrict access to finance, the majority of firms cut their marketing budgets. Therefore, marketing is one the most affected by crises.

Each year, the world's largest publicly traded global companies are listed on the Fortune Global 500 list. A total 87.5% of the companies in the Fortune Global 500 2018 list are from only nine countries (www.gfmag.com, 15.07.2019). Table 1 shows the countries' WEF global competitiveness index scores and the number of brands in the Fortune Global 500.

Table 1 compares the global competitiveness index of the countries and the number of brands in the Fortune Global 500 list by the WEF. The global competitiveness index consists of 12 components. Infrastructure includes services such as quality and maintenance of roads, electrical services and access to drinking water. The financial system includes services such as credit and insurance institutions, entrepreneurial capital. As it can be seen from the table, USA, which has the most global brand name, also has the highest score in the financial

Tab. 1: Comparison of Countries' Global Brand Quantities and Competitiveness Index

Country	Fortune Global 500 Count of Brand	Global Competitiveness Index Score – Rank	Infrastructure Score – Rank	Financial System Score – Rank
USA	126	85.6–1	89.5–9	92.1–1
China	120	72.6–28	78.1–29	71.9–30
Japan	52	82.5–5	91.5–5	86.4–10
Germany	32	82.8–3	90.2–7	80.2–21
France	28	78.0–17	90.1–8	82.9–17
South Korea	16	78.8–15	91.3–6	81.4–19
The Netherlands	15	82.4–6	92.4–4	83.7–16
Switzerland	14	82.6–4	93.3–3	89.4–4
Canada	12	79.9–12	80.6–25	86.1–11

system. In addition, USA has the highest score in transportation infrastructure scores. These data show that infrastructure and financial system play an important role in marketing finance.

1.1 Financial Barriers to Marketing

According to Ruytel and Wetzels (2000), there are three barriers between marketing and finance. First, the biggest problem between marketing and finance is the focus on different stakeholders. Marketing focuses on parties that are elemental in the market such as customers, suppliers, and competitors. Finance focuses on capital-providing stakeholders and institutions. The second is brand valuation. When evaluating the brand names, marketing can take different results from the financial unit since consumer-oriented factors are taken into consideration. Thirdly, while determining the capital budget, the finance department focuses on net present value, and the marketing department focuses on uncertainty and competitors in the market. Nonfinancial investments such as social responsibility projects and image studies are considered important by the marketing department. Fourth, when the working capital is determined, marketing managers focus on high inventory levels, while the finance department focuses on liquidity. The marketing department give importance to high inventory in order to respond more effectively to consumer demands.

Another financial barrier to marketing is the disruptions that may occur in the supply chain. This is called supply chain risk. Supply chain risk management (SCRM) is "the management of supply chain risks through coordination or collaboration among the supply chain partners so as to ensure profitability and continuity" (Tang, 2006). In the supply chain, risk arises when customer demands are met from unreliable and uncertain resources (Tang & Musa, SCRM, 2011). In order to manage risk, precautions such as paying attention to the selection of suppliers, creating product diversity, and sharing information throughout the supply chain are taken. Since strategically service firms are not dependent on a single supplier, they are not affected as much as manufacturers (Bloom & Schoenherr, 2011). Manufacturers develop SCRM as a precaution against interruptions in supply points.

Working capital is one of the other financial barriers to marketing. Working capital includes the assets provided for sustaining of the activity of an enterprise and the short-term resources used to finance them. Many companies in developing countries are experiencing problems not only with increasing costs but also due to untimely or inadequate working capital affecting all production operations. In Tesfo and Lutz (2006)'s literature review about barriers to

international trade, studies conducted in countries such as Venezuela, Kenya, and Turkey demonstrated that exporters mostly face high credit cost problems. This situation causes exporters to lose price advantage in the target market. As a result, it is a barrier to marketing.

2 Marketing Infrastructure

When firms do business internationally, marketing department plan product, price promotion, and distribution variables. There are basically two types of decisions about these variables. The first is to enter all countries over the world with a standard marketing mix. Although standardization is often used in technology products, it requires the presence of consumers with uniform global cultural characteristics. Portable MP3s create a new music culture all over the world. The second is the adaptation of these variables according to each country over the world. For example, the introduction of global fast food chains with customized product such as vegetable hamburger into the Indian market as it is a vegetarian country. On the other hand, conditions of the marketing infrastructure of the country is also important in controlling these variables in international marketing (Manrai et al., 2001). The availability of a country's infrastructure, such as distribution and logistics, is important to adapt to local conditions.

Infrastructure is the basic physical systems of an enterprise or a country. Water, electricity, and communication systems are examples of infrastructure (investopedia.com, 13.07.2019). Marketing infrastructure is the basic physical system that can carry out marketing activities. These are logistics systems, advertising and promotion agencies, internet, communication systems, intermediaries, and individuals (Fig. 3).

Logistics is delivering the materials, parts, and finished products to be used at the right place, at the right time, in the right amount, to the right customer, and under the right conditions in accordance with customer requirements. Aims of logistics are as follows:

- Do everything right the first time
- Apply six right principles in logistics (quantity, condition, place, time, customer, and price)
- Logistics is related to the benefits of space and time provided by distribution channels
- Good order management is essential
- Ensuring that the flow and storage in the supply chain is coordinated as a whole.

Fig. 3: Marketing Infrastructure

Logistics is examined in two classes as production and retail. The retail logistics forms the marketing infrastructure. Retail logistics consists of third-party logistics providers, service providers, and warehouse services. Logistics infrastructure providers include the following:

- Airport
- Sea port
- Railway station
- Logistics parks.

Logistics service providers include the following:

- Carriers and forwarders
- Courier, express, parcel, and postal service providers (CEP)
- System service providers and contracted logistics service providers

TNT, UPS, FedEx, and DPWN are the four largest logistics service providers in the world. Small logistics companies have small market shares. In addition, warehousing and warehouse management are vital for marketing infrastructure.

- Determine the level of customer service
- Ensure that demand for certain products (textile-fashion) is continuous
- The lead time is longer than order fulfillment
- Help balance supply and demand
- Balance production.

Large companies have sufficient budget to finance many marketing activities, such as transporting, storing, stocking, guarantee, and after-sales services. However, small- and medium-sized firms do not have sufficient budget due to financial difficulties. Therefore, small- and medium-sized companies are not involved in the process after production (Korkmaz, 2003). They transport their products to their customers through the distribution channel owned and managed by the intermediaries.

3 Marketing Risks

Although large firms have more capabilities in accessing finance than smaller ones, they may not be as successful in managing risks. Of course selling is important in doing business. But marketing is not just about selling. The main variables that affect the sustainability of the firm such as customer communication, brand image, advertising, and customer relationship management are also managed by marketing. At each stage of these processes, companies may face certain risks. These are called marketing risks, brand risk, product development risk, demand risk, concentration, price, distribution, operation, reputation, and sales (simplicable.com, 19.07.2019) (Fig. 4).

Brand risk is a term used when a brand has low brand value and a low level of awareness from its competition. New product development is the inability to hold new products in the market. Demand risk is the inability of products to meet the needs and demands of the customers. Concentration risk is the risk due to the very small number of customers bringing in most of the revenue. Price risk is that a brand cannot reach the desired price level due to intense competition. Distribution risk consists of channel conflict, loss of partners, and inventory risk. Operational risk arises due to the problems experienced in basic business processes such as production and distribution. Reputation risk is the risk of reputation damage due to negative events, such as poor customer service.

Fig. 4: Marketing Risks

Sales risk is the risk associated with sales processes, such as the resignation of a high-performance salesperson.

4 Marketing Entrepreneurship

Entrepreneurship is an economic and innovative activity to fill the gap created by demand that is not met in the market with certain expectations. According to Cantillon, entrepreneurial venture is investing in an uncertain future and expecting profit. According to Jean-Baptiste Say, one of the first to define entrepreneurship, entrepreneurship is an intermediary between labor and capital and to process economic resources with high efficiency. An entrepreneur is the person who takes the risk and carries out the operation to carry out an economic activity.

Entrepreneurial marketing is especially for start-up companies to develop innovative ideas in marketing to achieve maximum impact with limited resources. Entrepreneurs are often successful in marketing (Hills et al., 2008). In entrepreneurial marketing, new products and market opportunities are created through innovation of products, processes, and strategies. Successful

entrepreneurship is based on innovations with long-term orientation focused on customer desires and needs.

Large and financially strong firms can allocate sufficient budget for marketing investments and thus achieve successful marketing returns. However, start-ups have generally low number of employees and lack support from professional firms in marketing due to limited budget. Because of this reason, they often try to grow in the market where competitors cannot penetrate. These may include the presentation of customized products, such as personalized gifts. In addition, capturing special training videos to convince customers to try the product is widely used. Entrepreneurial marketing practices often use guerrilla marketing strategies that are cheap and effective. In addition to this, digital marketing strategies that enable reaching out to the masses through the internet as a fast communication channel are among the strategies used by marketing entrepreneurship.

Entrepreneurship and marketing play an important role in the development of countries. Entrepreneurship leads to the emergence of innovations in the economy and thus to increase in economic activities. Marketing promotes entrepreneurship and helps establish small businesses (Drucker, 1958). The marketing system serves as a bridge between entrepreneurs and managers. It enables the efficient use of marketing intermediaries in the economy and enables products to be delivered to customers quickly and inexpensively. Marketing triggers the increase in economic activities by turning secondary demand into effective demand. In addition, marketing raises standards and builds trust on consumers and thus increases the impact of firms on them. Table 2 shows entrepreneurship scores by country.

It shows the scores of countries according to the entrepreneurship index. USA with the highest entrepreneurial score is also one of the countries where developed competitiveness and financial system and hence marketing applications are best of the world. For example, in digital marketing, start-ups mostly origin from USA. It can be said that the countries that are most ideal for entrepreneurship are also ideal for marketing.

Conclusion

This chapter examines how the financial system of a country can affect the success of marketing. The study revealed that global brands emerged in developed countries with efficient financial system, high competition, improved infrastructure, and improved entrepreneurship. All of these variables are important affective marketing factors such as communication, customer relations, and image. Therefore, it can be said the stronger the financial system in a country, the lower

Tab. 2: Countries' Entrepreneurship Scores. Source: The Global Entrepreneurship and Development Institute

Countries	Score	Rank	Countries	Score	Rank
USA	83.6	1	Hong Kong	67.3	13
Switzerland	80.4	2	Austria	66.0	14
Canada	79.2	3	Germany	65.9	15
UK	77.8	4	Israel	65.4	16
Australia	75.5	5	Belgium	63.7	17
Denmark	74.3	6	Taiwan	59.5	18
Iceland	74.2	7	Chile	58.5	19
Ireland	73.7	8	Luxembourg	58.2	20
Sweden	73.1	9	Norway	56.6	21
France	68.5	10	Qatar	55.0	22
The Netherlands	68.1	11	Estonia	54.8	23
Finland	67.9	12	Korea	54.2	24
			Slovenia	53.8	25

the marketing risks. Entrepreneurship will be high in countries where marketing risks are low.

This chapter also examines the relationship between entrepreneurship and marketing. In the academic literature, entrepreneurship is generally defined as establishing a business in a field of uncertain future with the expectation of a return on profit. The relationship between entrepreneurship and marketing is about creating a customer base and understanding market dynamics of start-ups.

Marketing is a useful business activity for both companies and society. It has important contributions to the creation of ideal conditions for competitiveness and entrepreneurship for the society. For companies, establishing close relations with customers is one of the main tasks of marketing. Thus, it enables companies to understand their customers and increase their profitability. However, it is necessary to allocate sufficient resources to establish a marketing department within the company or to carry out marketing professionally. In particular, marketing is vital for start-ups to contact new customers. Actually there is no direct relationship between marketing and financial system. Both of these are interested in different topics. However, both have indirect relations as they encourage economic development and firm growth. For example, in developed economies with a strong financial system, infrastructure is also improved; and the company needs to spend less on marketing. As a result, marketing and entrepreneurship are carried out at high rates in developed economies. This shows that there is

a bilateral interdependent relationship where the financial system is disrupted when marketing is disrupted.

Bibliography

Beck, T. (2002). Financial development and international trade: Is there a link?. *Journal of international Economics, 57*(1), 107–131.

Blome, C., & Schoenherr, T. (2011). Supply chain risk management in financial crises—A multiple case-study approach. *International journal of production economics, 134*(1), 43–57.

Braun, M. (2003). *Financial contractibility and assets' hardness*. mimeo, University of California Los Angeles.

Chappelow, J. (2019). Infrastructure, In: *investopedia.com*, URL: https://www.investopedia.com/terms/i/infrastructure.asp, Access date: 13.07.2019.

De Ruyter, K., & Wetzels, M. (2000). The marketing–finance interface: A relational exchange perspective. *Journal of Business Research, 50*(2), 209–215.

Drucker, P. F. (1958). Marketing and economic development. *Journal of Marketing, 22*(3), 252–259.

Finansal Kriz Nedir? (N.D.). In: *anapara.com*, URL: https://anapara.com/finansal-kriz-nedir/, Access date: 25.06.2019.

Hills, G. E., Hultman, C. M., & Miles, M. P. (2008). The evolution and development of entrepreneurial marketing. *Journal of Small Business Management, 46*(1), 99–112.

Korkmaz, S. (2003). Küçük ve Orta Ölçekli İşletmelerin (KOBİ) Pazarlama ve Finansman Sorunlarının Çözümünde Risk Sermayesinin Kullanılabilirliği Üzerine Bir Araştırma. *Ticaret ve Turizm Eğitimi Fakültesi Dergisi, 2*(1), 233–258.

Manrai, L. A., Manrai, A. K., & Lascu, D. N. (2001). A country-cluster analysis of the distribution and promotion infrastructure in Central and Eastern Europe. *International Business Review, 10*(5), 517–549.

Spacey, J. (2017). 9 Types of Marketing. In: *simplicable.com*, URL https://simplicable.com/new/marketing-risk, Access Date: 19.07.2019.

Tang, C. S. (2006). Perspectives in supply chain risk management. *International Journal of Production Economics, 103*(2), 451–488.

Tang, O., & Musa, S. N. (2011). Identifying risk issues and research advancements in supply chain risk management. *International Journal of Production Economics, 133*(1), 25–34.

Tenekecioğlu, B., & Ersoy, F. (1999). *Makro Pazarlama*. Eskişehir: Birlik Ofset.

Tesfom, G., & Lutz, C. (2006). A classification of export marketing problems of small and medium sized manufacturing firms in developing countries. *International Journal of Emerging Markets*, *1*(3), 262–281.

Ventura, L. (2018). World's largest companies 2018. In: *gfmag.com*, URL: https://www.gfmag.com/global-data/economic-data/largest-companies, Access Date: 15.07.2019.

Ramazan Sayar

Chapter Two: The Relationship of Financial Development and Export; the Case of Turkey: A Literature Review[1]

Abstract: During the global financial crisis in 2008, the world trade experienced a large and severe collapse. Between 2008 and 2009, world exports and exports in Turkey decreased by 16% and 22%, respectively. The recent research has shown that the slowdown in global demand and tight financing conditions are the main factors behind this drop in exports. Auboin (2009) has stated that the 10%–15% decline in international trade after the global financial crisis may be due to the decline in commercial finance. In addition, the decline in commercial finance is particularly important for developing countries that have many sectors dependent on external financing. This study examines the reasons of the decline in exports in the world especially in Turkey during global financial crisis and assesses whether the financing constraints have contributed to this collapse.This study considered as a literature review consists of theoretical framework of the relationship between export and export financing. In order to show whether there is an effect of financing in international trade, firstly, research on the financial models is included in the classical models of international trade that show the dependence of international trading companies to financing. Secondly it has been utilized studies that analyzing of empirical evaluations of the effects of the external trade firms' dependence on external financing.

Keywords: Financial development, export financing, international trade, financial crisis

Introduction

This literature review study consists of theoretical framework of the relationship between export and export financing. In order to show whether there is an effect of financing in international trade, firstly, research on the financial models is included in the classical models of international trade that show the dependence of international trading companies to financing. Secondly it has been utilized studies that analyzing of empirical evaluations of the effects of the external trade firms' dependence on external financing.

---

1 This chapter is extracted from my doctorate dissertation, under the supervision of Prof. Dr. A. Yasemin Yalta, entitled "The Relationship between Export and Export Financing: The Case of Turkey" (PhD Dissertation, Hacettepe University, Ankara/ Turkey, 2018).

Auboin (2009) has stated that the 10%–15% decline in international trade after the global financial crisis may be due to the decline in commercial finance. In addition, the decline in commercial finance is particularly important for developing countries that have many sectors dependent on external financing. In this issue, primarily, the panel data studies that consist of more than one country available in the literature, then the country-based studies, and finally the studies related to Turkey are examined.

1 Literature

In this part of the study, the related studies in the literature will be examined theoretically and empirically. The studies about Turkey will be discussed after the empirical literature.

1.1 Theoretical Literature

In this section, firstly, the relationship between export and export financing is examined in theoretical framework. In order to show whether there is an effect of financing in international trade, firstly, how the dependence of international trading companies to finance is included in the classical models of international trade has been investigated. Then empirical evaluation studies of the effects of the external financing dependency of the exporting firms are examined.

While mentioning the theoretical framework, the studies that draw on the theories of Ricardo and Heckscher-Ohlin Samuelson, which are used as a starting point in the literature, draw attention. These studies aim to determine the impact on international trade flows of the financial sector by adding the concept of financial dependence on the theory in question. Thus, they used the international trade models developed by them with two countries and two sectors and found that the differences in financial development revealed comparative advantages. The most important aspect of these theoretical contributions is the assumption that the financial requirements and financial dependency of the two sectors are different in each country.

In the literature, firstly, Kletzer and Bardhan (1987) put forward that the development in financial sectors is the determinant of the comparative advantage of a country especially in the sectors dependent on finance. Kletzer and Bardhan (1987) showed that the exports of sectors[2] dependent on commercial

---

2 Especially sectors which need trade finance dependent for working capital requirements.

finance were affected negatively in the model they developed by including the financial sector in the Heckscher-Ohlin trade model, even in countries with the same technology and equipment. Therefore, the countries that develop the financial sector will gain comparative advantage by specializing in industries dependent on external financing. On the other hand, countries that do not develop the financial sector and therefore suffer from financing will have comparative advantage in sectors with less need for external financing. In the literature, studies were made in this direction by Qiu (1999), Beck (2002), and Becker et al. (2012).

The model developed by Baldwin (1989), which also takes into account the risk diversification function of financial systems, shows that the foreign trade model between the two countries mainly depends on the differences in their financial development. According to this model, a country with a developed financial system specializes in risky products, whereas vice versa specializes in risk-free products.

On the other hand, Do and Levchenko (2007), approaching the issue from the opposite point of view of Kletzer and Bardhan (1987), examine the effect of comparative advantage in international trade on the financial development level of a country. According to the authors, the demand for external financing of countries with comparative advantage in financing dependent goods increases, thus accelerating financial development. Therefore, if the comparative advantage in trade affects a country's production patterns, those which are more dependent on finance than those affected countries will be more willing to external finance and therefore have a high level of financial development. The study shows that trade directly affects financial development.

Chaney (2008) in the study of Krugman's (1980) model by adding the differentiation of firms to the concept of efficiency stated that they play a key role in the firm's export decision. The study has been said companies which has normally medium level productivity, they can potentially stand on their feet in foreign markets. On the other hand, he stated that firms cannot meet the their sunk cost because they cannot get enough profits; they are negatively affecting export because of financial constraints too.

Taylor (2010), who considers the financial difficulties experienced by exporters as a special cost, imposes financial constraints on the heterogeneous firm trade model developed by Melitz (2003). Trade openness also increases the average productivity in the economy and causes prices to decline, so firms with less productivity are forced to exit production because they cannot compete. At this point, the increase in financial development facilitates access to finance by limited firms in terms of financing and enables them to protect and even increase their production, thus making it easier for domestic firms to export. Decreasing

financial constraints of domestic firms decreases prices; and thus, there is going to development from low production capacity firms to high yield firms.

Fan et al. (2015) developed heterogeneous firm theory of Melitz (2003) by adding quality selection and credit constraints. They have not been investigated the effects of credit restrictions on the most appropriate quality and price choices of the firm's was motivation for the authors because of conduct this study. To test the model they developed, they measured firms' access to bank loans on a provincial basis during the sample period by collecting data on total bank loans, long-term bank loans, and short-term bank loans and taking the ratio of average bank loans to GDP. Using the Olley-Pakes and TFP method for the period 2000–2006 in their analysis of China's bank data, firm data, and Chinese customs data; they found that firms preferred to produce lower quality products when faced with tighter credit constraints. On the other hand, the authors state in the model that firms that do not prefer to reduce quality increase their prices.

The study of Dinopoulos et al. (2015) is similar to Fan et al. (2015)'s study. They have established a partial equilibrium model with internal quality, non-homothetic preferences and credit constraints. Their model was supported empirically by using a large data set of 2,169 Greek manufacturing companies in 2007, which included firm-level export, credit score, and financial variables. According to their OLS analysis findings, Greek exporters with less credit constraints have higher credit scores, higher export prices, higher export revenues, and export demand curves with less price elasticity. The positive and significant relationship between exporters with less credit constraints and export prices emerged in contradiction to the estimates of Melitz' (2003) type models. These models predict that firms constrained by less credit will face marginally low costs and lead to lower export prices. As a result of the analysis, it shows that credit constraints affect the exporter's behavior with changes in product quality.

In their theoretical studies, Bouët and Vaubourg (2016) investigate how financial constraints for sectors affect the export decisions of firms, if the form of competition within the sector is internal. Therefore, Neary and Tharakan (2012), as an extended version of the model, introduce financial constraint to a trade model that has an internal form of competition to explore the relationship between finance, investment, and trade. In this model, firms apply to external financing sources in their investments while increasing their production capacity. As a result of the study, it is found that the competitive behaviors of firms are very important to analyze the effect of financial factors on the firm's production capacity decision and export behaviors. The authors demonstrated that sector-level financial constraints not only increase firms' financial export

costs, but also increase the cost of investing in capacities. Moreover, they argue that the increase in the external financing cost affecting the export performance of firms creates a new financial shock transfer channel as the financial shock reduces the production capacity and exports of the firms. Although literature generally deals with the effects of financial factors on investment and trade separately, Bouët and Vaubourg (2016) have developed a comprehensive model that explains the decrease in firms' investments and exports due to the international financial crisis.

In the model developed by Chaney (2016) by adding liquidity constraints to the Melitz (2003) model, it was stated that financial constraints faced by potential exporters have a negative effect on trade flows. According to the author, even if companies have the potential to export, they cannot meet their entry costs due to the difficulty of reaching financial markets and cannot export. The main prediction of the model is that the lack of financial development has a preventive effect on exports. The model also suggests that the effect of exchange rates on trade flows will be reduced due to liquidity constraints. In other words, the valuation of the exchange rate has a decreasing effect on exports as it will weaken the competition, but at the same time the valuation of domestic assets indirectly reduces the liquidity constraint for exports. This study shows that liquidity constraints can change the behavior of exporters and the total export models. According to the author, liquidity constraints can also serve as links between markets and can cause crises to spread and grow.

In the studies abovesaid up to now, it is clearly seen that financial development can increase foreign trade due to the facilitating effect of firms on reaching the financing they need for export, but financial constraints have the opposite effect.

In the next section, the relationship between foreign trade and finance which has been examined theoretically so far will be explained with the studies in the applied literature.

1.2 Empirical Literature

Auboin (2009) said that the 10%–15% decline in international trade may be due to the decline in trade finance. In addition, the decline in commercial finance is particularly important for developing countries with more sectors dependent on external financing. Among the studies that are available in the literature on this subject, studies using panel data for more than one country are included in this section. Then, country-based studies will be included. At the end of the empirical literature, studies related to Turkey are included.

1.2.1 Panel Studies

In panel studies, studies that generally use macro data gain weight. The first study, Beck (2002), that empirically proves the hypotheses of Kletzer and Bardhan (1987) examined whether countries with more developed financial systems have a comparative advantage in industries using more external financing. Using a dynamic GMM model based on data from 65 countries between 1966 and 1995, the author examines the relationship between financial development and manufacturing industry trade. The theoretical model focuses on the role of financial intermediaries in facilitating large-scale and high-yield projects and demonstrates that economies with advanced financial sectors have a comparative advantage in the finance-dependent manufacturing industry. It demonstrates the causal relationship between financial development and trade in manufacturing goods by controlling country-specific effects and possible reverse causation advantage in the finance-dependent manufacturing industry. As a result of the analysis, it was found that the ratio of exports of finished goods, which are more dependent on foreign financing, to GDP and their share in total goods trade and the balance of foreign trade in finished goods are higher in countries which has high financial development level.

As one of the panel data studies, Ronci (2004) evaluates the impact of trade finance restriction on foreign trade in countries. In this study, 100 observations of 10 years of 10 crisis countries were used as panel data. The country's export and import volumes at the "t" time, world trade volume, world GDP index, relative GDP indices of exports and imports, short-term credits, and dummy variables were used as variables. Generalized Least Squares (GLS), Instrumental Variables (IV), and Generalized Method of Moments (GMM) tests have been used to analyze commercial finance; it had a positive effect on import and export volumes, income, and relative prices in the short term.

The study that applied the OLS methods covering 23 banking crises of Iacovane and Zavacka (2009), which examines the relationship between banking crises and exports, is based on the short-term data between the period 1980 and 2006 with 21 countries, consisting of developing and developed countries. According to the results of the analysis, they differentiated from the effects other than the financial shocks affecting exports; it was observed that the export-dependent sectors were more negative affected by the banking crisis than the other sectors, and the results were found to be significant.

Malouche (2009) evaluated the findings of the World Bank's survey in the first quarter of 2009, involving 425 firms and 78 banks from 14 developing

countries in 5 regions. The survey findings confirmed that the global financial crisis in developing countries constrained commercial finance for exporters and importers.

On the other hand, during crisis, stating that the effect of financing on the decline of trade is less than contrary to other studies, Korinek et al. (2010), using the GMM Arellano-Bond and Dynamic Panel Estimator methods, investigated the possible causes of the decrease in global trade between mid-2008 and the first quarter of 2009 in their studies involving 43 countries between 2005Q1 and 2009Q1. They examined changes in the access of trade finance (volume effect) and cost of trade finance (price effect) of foreign trade firms. In the short term, it showed the effect of commercial finance on the trade flow but stated that this effect was less than the effect of the decrease in demand. These important findings do not coincide with the literature which accepts that trade was only affected by financial conditions during the crisis.

Becker et al. (2012), who has results like Beck (2002), deals with annual bilateral trade flows between more than 170 countries, between 1970 and 1998. The fixed export costs were represented by the variables of the degree of standardization of the exported product, the distance between the exporting countries and the importing countries, the existence of a common border, and the existence of a common language between the two countries, respectively. Using the OLS regression model, he found that financial development encourages exports, and this effect is stronger in situations where fixed costs are high. All these findings show that financial development provides comparative advantage for sectors dependent on external financing.

The gravity model with variables of monthly USA production index, monthly bilateral exchange rate, two different commodity price indices, distance, seasonality, GDP, and financial crises, it has been concluded that the macroeconomic imbalance in African countries is mainly due to financial shocks that trade partners are exposed to. This result confirms the results of Kohler and Saville (2011). They showed that a banking crisis in the importing country had a negative effect on exports from Sub-Saharan Africa (SSA) countries even after one year, two years, and three years after the crisis. This is not only because of Africa's export composition and the density of primary products. The high level of dependence of African exporters on commercial finance leads to this effect. Therefore, in this study, it is emphasized that financial development can play an important role in coping with the effects of financial shocks in partner countries.

In this study, Hoffmann (2013) investigates the effects of the financing conditions on sectoral basis on export by using panel regression model with monthly data between 2002M1 and 2012M12 of EU countries. It also added financial fragilities to the analysis. The distinguishing aspect of this study is that it examines the credit conditions of the export countries as well as the different import countries. As a result of the study, while revealing the negative impact of the financial crisis on exports, it shows that its effects on exports are important determinants.

1.2.2 Country Basis Studies

Some country-based studies in the literature will be discussed in this section. The majority of these studies are microbased studies focusing on companies.

Firstly, Siregar (2010) examined the role of trade finance for each country in explaining the slowdown in export activities in Indonesia, Korea, and Thailand using ARDL test method with the data between the period 1993Q1 and 2009Q2. The findings confirm the indispensable role of trade credit in shaping the export flows of these three economies for 16 years. However, the effects of trade finance on export demand vary from one country to another. As expected, the negative consequences of the fall in trade credits on export performance are increasing during the financial crisis. This latest finding is remarkable in that it emphasizes the importance of the channels of transmission of the crisis from the financial sector to the real sector of the economy.

In the literature, as one of the studies demonstrating that commercial finance does not significantly affect exports, Levchenko et al. (2010) used OLS and a seemingly unrelated regression model with data of 6-digit NAICS sector America and their trade partners between the 2000Q1 and 2008Q4 quarters. They confirmed that America's trade with its trading partners around the world has declined significantly. They showed that the goods most affected by the commercial collapse were durable industrial goods and as much as capital goods. They found that there was greater decline in trade in sectors where domestic production declined at greater rates. Here, it is observed that especially the sectors using intermediate goods are more affected by the decrease in production, and there are big decreases in both exports and imports in terms of this sector. Later, they also tested the effect of commercial loans on exports, but assessed that there was no significant effect of commercial loans on exports and that export losses in sectors more dependent on commercial loans were not different from those that were less dependent.

Kohler and Saville (2011), one of the first studies to assess the impact of increased trade finance costs in connection with the global financial crisis, investigated the effects of trade finance constraints on trade performance in South Africa. The authors mention that stands out to the effect of demand effects of the financial crises on trade in the literature, and the authors try to explain the role of commercial finance in facilitating or complicating international trade. In the study, variables consisting of interbank lending rate, crises, real interest rate, and GDP for the period 2006–2010 were used in OLS and GLS regression analysis. As a result of their analysis, the authors found that the financial shocks exposed by their trading partners significantly reduced exports due to an increase in the interbank lending rate, which represented a contraction in commercial finance. Therefore, they concluded that the financial restriction resulting from the financial crises, which may have a serious impact on the export sector, caused fragility in the economies of developing countries such as South Africa.

One of the first studies to model the causal link between the financial sector and the commercial sector is the study of Amiti and Weinstein (2011). Using GMM Arellano-Bond, Dynamic Panel Estimator and OLS methods, the authors investigated the effect of banks' financial health on the exports of firms for the years 1990–2010 using the export data of some Japanese firms and the bank data that operated with these firms. The research provides evidence that a decline in the financial health of a bank indicates a decrease in exports for its customers. Moreover, the authors suggest that if the export forecast of firms is replaced with domestic sales, the financial health impact of banks is weaker. Their findings theoretically support the fact that the banking crisis has a more significant impact on international trade than domestic activities. The authors found that the financial shocks during the recent financial crisis caused Japan at least 20% of the overall decline in exports. This explains why the collapse in trade in 2009 was very severe compared to the decline in GDP.

In the study conducted by Minetti and Zhu (2011) using the survey method, the effects of credit restriction on export decisions and export sales of 4,680 Italian firms with more than 10 workers between 1998 and 2005 were tried to be estimated. In this study in which linear regression model is applied, export, credit constraint which is represented by control variables showing the financial position of firms, liquidity ratio, financial leverage ratio, and ratio of cash flow to total assets are used. The data for the restriction measurements were compiled from the responses to the questionnaire rather than the financial statements of the firms. As a result, it was found that the export preferences of firms with credit restrictions decreased by 39%, and their foreign sales decreased by more

than 38%. In addition, the negative effect of credit restriction on foreign sales was found to be significantly higher than domestic sales. Thus, firms in industries with high dependence on foreign credit have shown that their exports have decreased due to credit constraints; and moreover, credit shortages have hampered the export of high-tech sectors.

Chor and Manova (2012), one of the first studies to prove the effects of credit shrinkage on exports during the 2008 global financial crisis, used the panel regression model with America's monthly import data between November 2006 and October 2009. They also used the one-month interbank lending rates of 31 countries exporting to the United States as representatives for the cost of short-term trade financing. Chor and Manova (2012) investigated whether the negative impact of external financial dependence on the exports of sectors stemmed from the global credit tightening identified by high interbank lending rates, and the 2008 financial crisis variable represented by a dummy variable. In times of no crisis in the overall functioning of the economy, the interbank lending rate may be indicative of both limited credit access and excessive credit demand. In times of crisis, this increase is considered as an indicator of the decrease in credit supply. As a result of the analysis, it is shown that countries with high interbank lending rates export less to the US, especially in sectors that are highly dependent on external financing. This effect grew during the financial crisis. The results show that tight credit conditions in a country adversely affect exports as they provide firms with less and/or more expensive trade finance. In this study, this effect is more evident especially for sectors that are dependent on trade finance and therefore are most vulnerable to financial shocks. It is stated by the authors that the sectors that are heavily dependent on trade finance as well as those with limited access to trade credits or secured assets are affected more seriously.

Berman et al. (2012), in their study in which they used panel regression model, used as the representative the delivery time of the goods to determine the intensity of the financial problems of the firms. In the analysis conducted based on the data of French export companies in the period 1995–2005, during the financial crisis periods, the extension of the delivery time of the goods not only increased the working capital needs of the firms but also increased the likelihood of the importer not paying the debt. As a result of the study, when have been export countries by firms that included in the analysis are affected by a financial crisis, their exports decrease and the length of the delivery times to the ship becomes an indicator of the decrease in exports. In a paper reviewing the impact of financial shocks on commercial finance for Korea between "1999M1–2010M12" monthly periods and "2001Q1–2010Q4" quarterly periods, Hwang and Im (2013) talked

about the difficulty of reaching reliable data for measuring trade finance. Then, unlike the variables used in the literature, he conducted a VAR analysis by using the foreign trade credits offered by commercial banks and the documentary bill variables purchased. In this study, it was found that financial shocks negatively affected trade finance due to changes in financial variables.

Bardakas (2014), in his study on the export of Greece between 2000 and 2012, investigated the relationship between firms' access to finance and their exports by using Johansen multivariate integration technique. As a result of the analysis, it is seen that both the short- and long-term firm financing positively affects the export performance considering the adverse causality effect. In his research, the author calculated that a 10% decrease in firm financing led to a decrease in exports of 6%–9% in the short term. On the other hand, it is determined that a 10% increase in the financing provided by banks to firms during the enlargement process will result in an increase of 6%–9% in exports so it will have an effect 1%–2% on the growth rate consequently.

Feenstra et al. (2014) in their study, which analyzed Chinese firms' data by the Extended Olley-Pakes (1996) method between 2000 and 2008, found that in an environment in which banks could not observe the productivity of firms, credit restrictions for domestic and exporting firms emerged. In the study, it was observed that in such cases, banks lend less short-term debt than the amount needed by firms for production; however, it is stated that exporters who need a longer period of time for export deliveries have more credit shortages than domestic firms. As a result, they found that as the export share of Chinese firms increased, as shipping times for export increased, and as the irregularity of productivity of firms which were identified some lack of information by banks, the credit restriction for these firms was more stringent.

Paravisini et al. (2014) analyzed Peru's bank credit data which firm basis between 2007 and 2009 years, in their study which used OLS, IV and probit models. They shows that the loan had a primary impact on the export volume of firms that continued to export to a specific product and target market in the 2008 crisis. But it also showed that the biggest determinant of Peru's exports was related to non-credit factors such as international demand and prices. In the study, it was stated that ignoring export determinants such as product type and destination other than bank credit may cause serious biased estimates in order to examine the effect of credit contraction on exports.

Between 1999 and 2007, Muûls (2015) using the Linear Probability Model analyzed the data set of Belgian manufacturing firms imports, exports, financing, and credit ratings and found that firms with lower credit constraints were more

likely to export or import. In addition, the study showed that credit restrictions affect imports and exports in different ways. For example, in exports, intense and wide margins in terms of products and destinations are decreasing along with credit constraints. In imports, only the intense margin in terms of product is significantly associated with credit constraints.

So far, studies on foreign trade and financing conducted worldwide and on the basis of countries have been examined. In the following section, as by need of our work the studies that about this issue is related to Turkey will be investigated.

1.2.3 Studies on Turkey

During the global financial crisis, as the first Turkey study of this area Acar (2009) used the questionnaire method and conducted the survey with 40 companies and five bank executives. According to the survey's findings, the reasons of firms' exporting barriers in Turkey are the foreign trade finance problems 10%, lack of foreign demand 60%, funding problems of import firms 40%. It is stated here that the exports of Turkish firms have decreased due to the decrease in foreign demand rather than foreign trade financing. The reason for the decrease in foreign demand was the financing problems of importing companies. It is seen that the decrease in exports is related to the problems experienced by the importer. The study seems similar to the results of Kohler and Saville (2011) and Berman et al. (2012).

Degirmen and Gundogdu (2010) used the annual data of firms among the first thousand industrial enterprises between 1997 and 2008 in their studies on the financing preferences of export companies. In this study, Pedroni Panel Co-integration Test was conducted by using the variables such as the ratio of firms' exports to total sales, the growth rate of short- and long-term loans, and capital growth rate. As a result of the analysis, a significant relationship was found between the variables in the long term.

Akarım (2013) based on the data of the Istanbul Stock Exchange in the 2000–2011 period, using the panel logit analysis model, tested the validity of financial constraint hypothesis for Turkey. As a result, Akarım (2013) found a significant relationship between firm bigness, financial constraints and the possibility export, but study has revealed that there is no validity of the financial constraint hypothesis for Turkey. Thus, it has been shown that increasing the scale of export firms by time gradually decreases their financial constraints.

Türkcan (2016), in his study on data analysis and interpretation on payment methods in international trade, states that being in the global market

poses many risks to the exporting companies that are not active in the domestic market. He also stated that the functioning of commercial finance and commercial financing mechanisms helps to soften or mitigate the risks associated with doing business internationally for exporters and importers. This study reveals the structure and development of payment methods in international trade and the impact of 2008–2009 global financial crisis on these compositions. Turkey's bilateral trade with 206 countries during the period 2002–2012 financing data is used. Three important determinations were made in this study. First of all, while Turkey's exports mainly financed with open account method, the majority of imports were carried out with the cash advance method. Second, trade finance among firms in Turkey (open accounts and advance payments) increased dramatically during the period 2002–2012; on the other hand, share of the medium-term trade finance (letters of credit documents and money) decreased. Finally, both exporters and importers started to use the cash advance method, which is the safest method, more intensively than the other methods shortly after the global recession in 2008. In general, the models presented in this article demonstrate that Turkish companies engaged in international trade cannot determine the appropriate payment methods for themselves but also assume all risks associated with international trade transactions.

Bülbül and Demiral (2016) looked at the causality relationships between exports, Eximbank loans and economic growth by using quarterly data for 2002–2015. As a result of the analysis using Johansen cointegration test and Granger causality test, a two-way causality was found between export and economic growth. But one-way causality was found from export to Eximbank loans. Furthermore, no long-term relationship was found between exports and loans.

The results obtained in the empirical literature presented above are summarized in Tab. 1.

Conclusion

As a result of this study, it is seen that there are few studies in the literature investigating the relationship between foreign trade and finance. Moreover, most of the current studies have used linear models assuming that the relationship between foreign trade and finance is linear. The studies on the relationship between foreign trade and finance by nonlinear models, based on the literature suggesting that the determinants of exports will vary during crises, will fill this gap in the literature.

Tab. 1: Applied Literature

Panel Made with data Method Works	The Dependent Variable	Financing Criteria	Period and Countries	Method	Results
Beck (2002)	Finished Goods Exports	Ratio of Private Sector Loan to GDP	65 countries between 1966 and 1995	GMM Model	In countries with high levels of financial development, the ratio of exports of finished goods more dependent on foreign financing to GDP and its share in total goods trade, and the trade balance in finished goods were higher.
Ronci (2004)	Export and Import Volume of Countries	Short-Term Loans	100 observations from 10 countries for 10 years	GLS, IV, GMM Tests	Commercial finance had a positive effect on import and export volumes, income, and relative prices in the short term.
Iacovone and Zavacka (2009)	Industry Export Growth	Bank Finance, Commercial Loans, and Tangible Assets at Industry Level	Between 1980 and 2006 21 countries	OLS	It was found that export-dependent sectors were more adversely affected by the banking crisis than other sectors.
Korinek et al. (2010)	Import and Total Trade	Export Credit Insurance, 10-Year Government Bond Rates	Between 2005Q1–2009Q1 43 countries	GMM Arellano-Bond, Dynamic Panel Estimator	In the short term, it showed the effect of commercial finance on the trade flow but stated that this effect was less than the effect of the decrease in demand.
Becker et al. (2012)	Export	Accounting Standards and Ratio of Private Loans to GDP	Between 1970 and 1998 more than 170 countries	OLS	It shows that financial development provides comparative advantage for sectors dependent on external financing.
Hoffmann (2013)	Export of the European Region	Euribor Ratios, Assets, Commercial Credit Availability, Liquidity Ratio, and Debt Ratio	2002M1–2012 M12 between EU Countries	Panel Regression Model	The high cost of commercial finance and the difficulties in reaching credit lead to a decrease in export volume.

Country Analysis	The Dependent Variable	Financing Criteria	Period and Countries	Method	Results
Levchenko et al. (2010)	Import Export	Interbank Lending Rate	Between 2000Q1 and 2008Q4 America	OLS and Apparently Unrelated Regression Model	They also tested the effect of commercial loans on exports, but assessed that there was no significant effect of commercial loans on exports, and that export losses in sectors more dependent on commercial loans were not different from those that were less dependent.
Siregar (2010)	Export of Countries	Commercial Loans	1993 Q1–2009Q2 between Indonesia, Korea, and Thailand	ARDL Test	The negative consequences of the fall in trade credits on export performance are increasing during the financial crisis.
Minetti and Zhu (2011)	Export	Credit Restriction, Liquidity Ratio, and Leverage Ratio	Between 1998–2005 Years, 4680 Italian Companies	Linear Regression Model	They found that firms in industries with high dependence on foreign credit decreased their exports due to credit constraints; and moreover, they prevented exports of high-tech sectors with high levels of credit dependence.
Kohler and Saville (2011)	Export of South Africa	Interbank Lending Rate	Year 2006–2010 to RAI South Africa	OLS, GLS	They found that their trading partners under the influence of the financial shocks due to an increase in the interbank lending rate significantly reduced exports.
Amiti and Weinstein (2011)	Export of Companies	Market Value Book Value Ratio of Banks	Japanese Firms Between 1990 and 2010	GMM Arellano-Bond, Dynamic Panel Estimator, OLS	The research provides evidence that a decline in the financial health of a bank indicates a decrease in exports for its customers.

(*continued on next page*)

Tab. 1: (continued)

Country Analysis	The Dependent Variable	Financing Criteria	Period and Countries	Method	Results
Berman, De Sousa, Martin and Mayer (2012)	Export	Delivery Time of Export Goods to Ship	1 French Export Firm Between 1995 and 2005	Panel Regression Model	When the countries that the firms which included in the analysis export to are affected by a financial crisis, their exports decrease and the length of the delivery time to ship becomes an indicator of the decrease in exports.
Chor and Manova (2012)	Imports	Exporter Country Interbank Lending Interest Rate, Foreign Finance Dependency, Trade Credit Density	2006 M11–2009 M10 Cross America	Panel Regression Model	It shows that tight credit conditions in a country adversely affect exports as they provide firms with less and/or more expensive trade finance.
Hwang and Im (2013)	Commercial Finance	Documentary Policy, Foreign Trade Loans	1999M1–2010M 12 2001Q1–2010Q4 Korea	VAR Model	In this study, it was found that financial shocks negatively affected trade finance due to changes in financial variables.
Bardakas (2014)	Demanded Export Volume	Special Loans Granted by Banks to Nonfinancial Production	Greece Between 2000 and 2012	Johansen Multivariate Integration Technique	As a result of the analysis, it is seen that both the short- and long-term firm financing positively affects the export performance considering the adverse causality effect.

Feenstra, Li, and Yu (2014)	Export	Credit Restriction, Interest Payments of Firms	160,000 Chinese Manufacturer from 2000 to 2008	Extended Olley-Pakes (1996)	They found that as the export share of Chinese firms increased, as shipping times for export increased, and as the irregularity of productivity of firms whose were identified some lack of information by banks, the credit restriction for these firms was more stringent.
Paravini et al. (2014)	Export	Credit Supply of Banks	6169 Peru Export Company Between 2007 and 2009	OLS, IV, Probit Models	It shows that the loan had a primary impact on the export volume of firms that continued to export to a specific product and target market in the 2008 crisis. But it also showed that the biggest determinant of Peru's exports was related to non-credit factors such as international demand and prices.
Muûls (2015)	Export and Import Volumes	Financing and Credit Ratings	Belgian Manufacturing Companies Between 1999 and 2007	Linear Probability Model	It has been found that firms with lower credit restrictions are more likely to export or import.
Turkey to Work Things	**The Dependent Variable**	**Financing Criteria**	**Period and Countries**	**Method**	**Results**
Degirmen and Gundogdu (2010)	Ratio of Exports of Companies to Total Sales	Growth Rate of Short-Term Bank Loans, Growth Rate of Long-Term Bank Loans, and Capital Growth Rate	The First Thousand Industrial Establishments Between 1997 and 2008	Pedroni Panel Co-integration Test	In the long run, a significant relationship was found between the ratio of firms' exports to total sales, the growth rate of short- and long-term loans, and capital growth rate. According to the results, firms use both banks and capital markets to finance their exports. Of these, they mostly prefer short-term bank loans.

(*continued on next page*)

Tab. 1: (continued)

Turkey to Work Things	The Dependent Variable	Financing Criteria	Period and Countries	Method	Results
Bülbül and Demiral (2016)	Export	Eximbank Loans	Quarterly Data for the Years 2002–2015	Johansen Cointegration Test and Granger Causality Test	There was a two-way causality between exports and economic growth and a one-way causality from exports to Eximbank loans. Furthermore, no long-term relationship was found between exports and loans.
Turkcan (2016)	Binary Trade Finance Data		Period 2002–2012; 206 countries with Turkey	Data Analysis and Interpretation	In the results of the study, mainly in Turkey's exports were financed with open account method, trade finance among firms in the trade Turkey (open accounts and advance payments) increased dramatically during the period 2002–2012, on the other hand, share of the medium-term trade finance (letters of credit documents and money) decreased. Finally, both exporters and importers started to use the cash advance method, which is the safest method, more intensively than the other methods shortly after the global recession in 2008.

Bibliography

Acar, O. (2009). *Türkiye'de dış ticaret ve dış ticaretin finansmanı durum değerlendirmesi*. TEPAV, http://www.tepav.org.tr/tur/admin/dosyabul/upload/TRTEPAVTicaretin%20Finansmani%20Raporu.pdf, Access Date: 27.06.2019.

Akarım, Y. D. (2013). The impact of financial factors on export decisions: The evidence from Turkey. *Economic Modelling, 35*, 305–308. doi:10.1016/j.econmod.2013.06.038

Amiti, M., & Weinstein, D. E. (2011). Exports and financial shocks. *The Quarterly Journal of Economics, 126*(4), 1841–1877.

Auboin, Marc (2009): Restoring trade finance during a period of financial crisis: Stocktaking of recent initiatives, WTO Staff Working Paper, No. ERSD-2009-16, World Trade Organization (WTO), Geneva, http://dx.doi.org/10.30875/4de92d90-en.

Baldwin, R. (1989). Exporting the capital markets: Comparative advantage and capital market imperfections. In D. Audretsch, L. Sleuwaegen, & H. Yamawaki (Eds.), *The convergence of international and domestic markets*. Amsterdam: North-Holland.

Bardakas, I. C. (2014). *Financing exports of goods: A constraint on Greek economic growth*. Working Paper178, Bank of Greece, Athens.

Beck, T. (2002). Financial development and international trade: Is there a link? *Journal of International Economics, 57*(1), 107–131.

Becker, B., Chen, J., & Greenberg, D. (2012). Financial development, fixed costs, and international trade. *The Review of Corporate Finance Studies, 2*(1), 1–28.

Berman, N., De Sousa, J., Martin, P., & Mayer, T. (2012). *Time to ship during financial crises*. Paper presented at the NBER International Seminar on Macroeconomics 2012.

Bouët, A., & Vaubourg, A.-G. (2016). Financial constraints and international trade with endogenous mode of competition. *Journal of Banking & Finance, 68*, 179–194. doi:https://doi.org/10.1016/j.jbankfin.2016.03.007

Bülbül, S. E., & Demiral, A. (2016). Türkiye Ekonomisinde Ekonomik Büyüme, İhracat Ve Exımbank Kredileri Arasındaki Nedensellik İlişkisi: 2002–2015. *Öneri Dergisi, 12*(46), 21–40.

Chaney, T. (2008). Distorted gravity: The intensive and extensive margins of international trade. *The American Economic Review, 98*(4), 1707–1721.

Chaney, T. (2016). Liquidity constrained exporters. *Journal of Economic Dynamics and Control, 72*, 141–154.

Chor, D., & Manova, K. (2012). Off the cliff and back? Credit conditions and international trade during the global financial crisis. *Journal of International Economics, 87*(1), 117–133.

Degirmen, S., & Gundogdu, Y. (2010). Türkiye'de Ihracat Yapan Firmalarin Finansman Stratejileri. *Business and Economics Research Journal, 1*(4), 1.

Dinopoulos, E., Kalyvitis, S., & Katsimi, M. (2015). *Export pricing and credit constraints: Theory and evidence from Greek Firms*. University of Florida, Mimeo.

Do, Q.-T., & Levchenko, A. A. (2007). Comparative advantage, demand for external finance, and financial development. *Journal of Financial Economics, 86*(3), 796–834.

Fan, H., Lai, E. L. C., & Li, Y. A. (2015). Credit constraints, quality, and export prices: Theory and evidence from China. *Journal of Comparative Economics, 43*(2), 390–416. doi:https://doi.org/10.1016/j.jce.2015.02.007

Feenstra, R. C., Li, Z., & Yu, M. (2014). Exports and credit constraints under incomplete information: Theory and evidence from China. *Review of Economics and Statistics, 96*(4), 729–744. doi:10.1162/REST_a_00405

Hoffmann, M. (2013). *The effect of the financial crisis on European exports the trade finance transmission channels* (Unpublished master thesis). Erasmus University Rotterdam.

Hwang, S., & Im, H. (2013). Financial shocks and trade finance: Evidence from Korea. *Economics Letters, 120*(1), 104–107. doi:10.1016/j.econlet.2013.04.005

Iacovone, L., & Zavacka, V. (2009). *Banking crises and exports: Lessons from the Past?* (World Bank Policy Research Working Paper 5016).

Kletzer, K., & Bardhan, P. (1987). Credit markets and patterns of international trade. *Journal of Development Economics, 27*(1–2), 57–70.

Kohler, M., & Saville, A. (2011). Measuring the impact of trade finance on country trade flows: A South African perspective. *South African Journal of Economic and Management Sciences, 14*(4), 466–478.

Korinek, J., J. Le Cocguic and P. Sourdin (2010), "The Availability and Cost of Short-Term Trade Finance and its Impact on Trade", OECD Trade Policy Working Papers, No. 98, OECD Publishing. doi: 10.1787/5kmdbg733c38-en.

Levchenko, A. A., Lewis, L. T., & Tesar, L. L. (2010). The collapse of international trade during the 2008–09 crisis: In search of the smoking gun. *IMF Economic Review, 58*(2), 214–253.

Malouche, M. (2009). *Trade and trade finance developments in 14 developing countries post September 2008—A World Bank Survey* (World Bank Policy Research Working Paper Series, 5138).

Melitz, M. J. (2003). The impact of trade on intra-industry reallocations and aggregate industry productivity. *Econometrica*, *71*(6), 1695–1725.

Minetti, R., & Zhu, S. C. (2011). Credit constraints and firm export: Microeconomic evidence from Italy. *Journal of International Economics*, *83*(2), 109–125. doi:10.1016/j.jinteco.2010.12.004

Muûls, M. (2015). Exporters, importers and credit constraints. *Journal of International Economics*, *95*(2), 333–343.

Neary, J. P., & Tharakan, J. (2012). International trade with endogenous mode of competition in general equilibrium. *Journal of International Economics*, *86*(1), 118–132.

Olley, S., & Pakes, A. (1996). The dynamics of productivity in the Telecommunications Equipment Industry, in "Econometrica", vol. 64.

Paravisini, D., Rappoport, V., Schnabl, P., & Wolfenzon, D. (2014). Dissecting the effect of credit supply on trade: Evidence from matched credit-export data. *The Review of Economic Studies*, *82*(1), 333–359.

Qiu, L. D. (1999). Credit rationing and patterns of new product trade. *Journal of Economic Integration*, *14*(1), 75–95.

Ronci, M. M. V. (2004). *Trade finance and trade flows: Panel data evidence from 10 crises*. Washington, DC: International Monetary Fund.

Siregar, R. Y. (2010). Trade financing and export performance: Experiences of Indonesia, Korea and Thailand. In C. Findlay, F. Parulian & J. Corbett (Eds.), *Linkages between real and financial aspects of economic integration in East Asia* (p. 226). Jakarta: ERIA.

Taylor, A. (2010). *Trade and financial sector reforms: Interactions and spillovers (5279)*. Retrieved from The World Bank https://openknowledge.worldbank.org/handle/10986/3766, Access Date: 27.09.2019.

Türkcan, K. (2016). Evolving patterns of payment methods in Turkish Foreign Trade. *World Journal of Applied Economics*, *2*(1), 3–29.

Yılmaz Onur Ari

Chapter Three: Interactive Effects of Remittances and Financial Development on Turkey's Economic Growth

Abstract: Labor migration from underdeveloped and developing countries to developed countries has gained great importance, especially with the acceleration of globalization since the 1980s. The remittances that migrants earn by working in the receiving countries and send to their families have become an important tool for fighting against poverty and supporting economic growth.Migrant remittances, which are more stable than other financial sources, became a primary source of foreign exchange for supporting economic growth of developing countries by financing the current account deficit, reducing poverty, increasing consumption expenditures, and increasing household savings and investments. Remittances, which are an important financial source for developing countries, affect the economic growth in the remittance-receiving country positively or negatively. There is no consensus in the literature about the effect of remittances on economic growth.Remittances take an important place for lowering poverty and supporting economic growth because Turkey is a developing country. In this study, I analyzed a historical background of remittance flows to Turkey. By looking back at the literature, I tried to correlate Turkish remittances to Turkish financial sector development.

Keywords: Remittances, migrant workers, labor flows, Turkish financial sector, economic growth, globalization

Introduction

Globalization affects growth and development through international trade, financial integration, and technological innovations. However, global labor flows that are the subject of this study have an important function in influencing growth and development. Particularly, a large number of people from less developed and developing countries have become aware of the large gap between the welfare world and their economic situation. The remittances sent to home country increase the purchasing power of inhabitants and enable them to integrate better to the world market.

Turkey is a developing country so remittances take an important place for reducing poverty, decreasing budget deficit, and increasing household income, just like for many other developing countries. After the mid-2000s, remittance flows to Turkey from Turkish migrants fall dramatically because of many reasons.

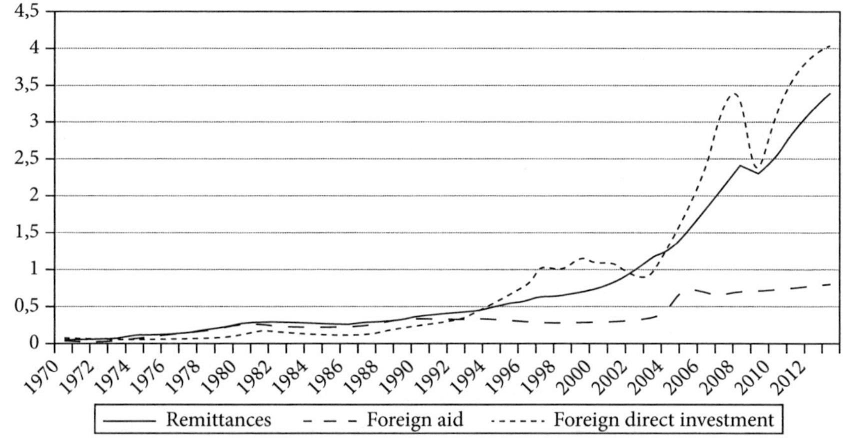

Fig. 1: Average Level of Remittances, Foreign Aid and FDI, 1970–2013 (billion dollars). Source: Eggoh, J., Bangake, C., & Semedo, G. (2019). Do remittances spur economic growth? Evidence from developing countries, *The Journal of International Trade & Economic Development*, 28(4), 391–418

Recently Turkey has been suffering from the lack of foreign exchange, hence the importance of remittances for Turkey's growth was emphasized in this study. Besides, theoretical arguments about how remittances affect growth through financial sector development were discussed.

1 International Migration, Remittances, and Economic Growth

Economic growth means the rate of growth of real per capita GDP. As a result of international capital inflows such as remittances through the activities of institutions in the financial system, the level of economic growth in a country can accelerate (Olaniyan, 2019: 23). The volume of the flow of remittances has been gradually increasing in recent years, and their effect on the receiving countries is attracting attention. According to the World Bank (2013), remittance flows to the developing countries have reached $ 414 billion in 2013 through the official channels plus unknown amounts transferred through unofficial channels. Remittances are now the second largest source of external financial flows behind foreign aid and showing an increasing trend especially after 2000 (Eggoh, Bangake & Semedov, 2019: 391) (Fig. 1).

At this point, international migration is able to make a positive impact for poverty reduction and development in the future. In fact, remittances can be a

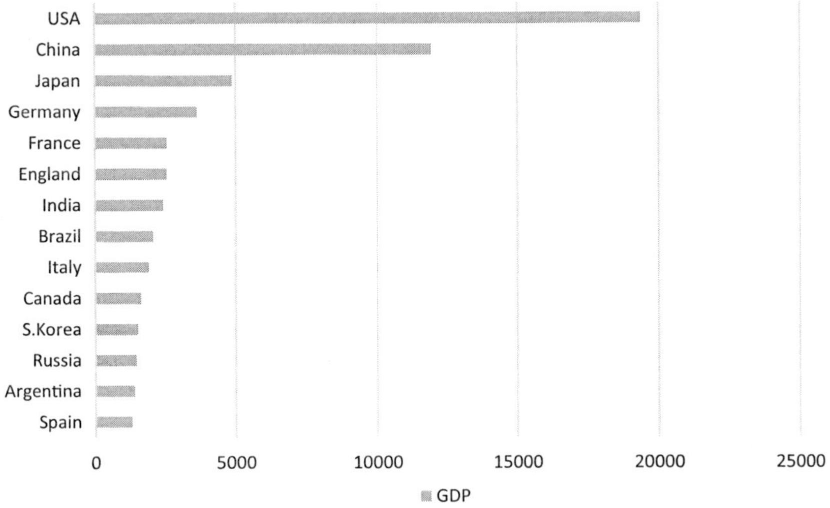

Fig. 2: Gross Domestic Product (GDP) Ranking by Country, 2017 (in billion US dollars). Source: https://www.statista.com/statistics/268173/countries-with-the-largest-gross-domestic-product-gdp/ (Retrieved on 01.07.2019)

strong subsistence strategy for many poor people, thus they can make a crucial contribution to national economic growth (Laczko, 2005: 11). Migrant workers play indeed an important role in developing countries (Zhang & Lin, 2010: 203). Migrant transfers, which are the financial equivalent of migration, are considered as the most concrete contributions of migrants to the development of origin or source regions (Vargas-Lundiu, Lanly, Villareal & Osorio, 2008: 6). Global labor flows contribute to the economic growth of underdeveloped and developing countries through remittances, and contribute to migrant-receiver developed countries through qualified labor migration. Figure 2 shows the top 15 highest GDP countries in 2017. The US economy is the world's largest economy with 19362.13 billion dollars. Developing countries such as Russia, India, China, Brazil, and Argentina were positively affected by the globalization process and achieved high growth rates. It can be argued that developing countries aiming at a stable and high rate of growth, increasing living standards, and reducing poverty need to implement policies to increase integration with the global world.

At this juncture, it is seen that migration flows, which are mentioned in growth theories as the motor power in shaping economic growth through knowledge and cross-border mobility of the labor force, have an economic and

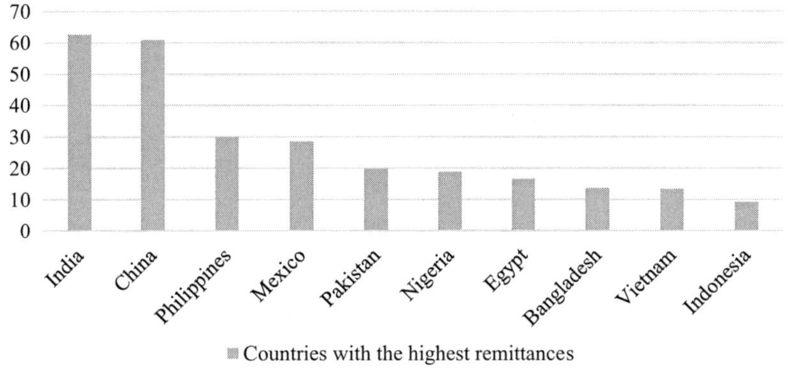

Fig. 3: Countries with the Highest Remittances, 2016 (billion dollars).
Source: KNOMAD (2017), Migration and Remittances: Recent Developments and Outlook, April 2017

social effect on both migrant sending and receiving countries. The degree of this impact varies depending on the labor force of the receiving and sending countries. Demographic and educational aspects of migration play a key role in measuring the contribution of migrants to growth or to assess whether migration has a positive impact on per capita income growth. If the receiving country attracts qualified labor force, it has positive effects on the economic growth, and on the other hand contributes to the economies of emigrants through foreign exchange revenues (Borjas, 1994: 1669; Boubtane, Dumont, & Rault, 2014: 2–4; Gupta & Chakraborty, 2006: 1–2). Rapidly growing sending countries such as India, China, and Mexico provide a significant part of their GDP through remittances sent by their citizens to their countries (Fig. 3).

There are many studies which are conducted to study the main determinants of workers' remittances in the developing countries. From a migrant worker's perspective, there are both microeconomic and macroeconomic purposes to remit. The marital status, family size, and social ties of a migrant with sending country represent microeconomic determinants. On the other hand, income and wage differences between sending and receiving countries, macroeconomic instability, and financial development are major macroeconomic motives to remit (Akçay, 2018: 895). I mentioned about the interactive effects of remittances and financial development on economic growth theoretically at the second part of this study.

Two main theories can be mentioned while analyzing the interactive effects of remittances and financial sector development on economic growth (Olaniyan,

2019: 23). According to the complementarity hypothesis, which was propounded by Mundaca (2009: 300), remittances and financial development support each other in promoting economic growth; and migrants can send money to their home countries cheaply, safely, and faster when there is a highly developed financial sector. Besides, it simplifies that the effects of remittances on economic growth seem to be more recognizable only in countries where banking systems function well. The hypothesis also argues that remittances infiltrate financial intermediaries to their beneficiaries in order to augment the well-being of the receivers and economic growth. According to substitutability hypothesis, which was asserted by Giuliano and Ruiz-Arranz (2009: 144), remittances can be an important source of financing growth-enhancing activities in countries which have less developed financial sectors. It also assumes that the effect of remittances on economic growth is more noticeable in less financially developed countries, where banks are weak in supporting adequate funds for potentially productive activities; therefore remittances act as substitutes for financial sector development.

2 The Effects of Remittances and Financial Sector on Economic Growth

The effects of remittances on economic growth, combined with the roles played by intermediaries in the financial sector, have continued to leave a huge impact and attention in the development literature (Olaniyan, 2019: 19). There are both positive and negative views about the growth effect of remittances in the literature.

Some studies assert positive causal links between remittances and growth. Researchers essentially state that remittances increase the disposable income of family members in home countries. Besides, these family members may increase their human capital levels in the long run by benefitting better health and education services. Also remittances provide a developed financial system and expedite economic growth. Acceleration of growth causes poverty reduction (Arı & Özcan, 2011: 104; Azam & Khan, 2011: 41; Guilano & Ruiz Arranz, 2009: 144; Kratou & Gazdar, 2016: 52).

From a positive perspective, remittances may increase investments and total factor productivity. Moreover, they would reduce poverty and improve the purchasing power. Recent studies mention about the relationship between private transfers and investment channels (Kratou & Gazdar, 2016: 52). Guilano and Ruiz Arranz (2009: 144) found that remittances can significantly increase economic growth depending upon the development of financial sector in a country,

accordingly showing that financial sector can be a channel through which remittances affect growth. They also analyze that financial sector and migrant workers' remittances can be substitutes. If a country has a well-developed financial sector, credit constraints are removed and remittances which migrants send their home country need not be used productively. However, in countries which have a poor financial system, remittances can be a crucial source of financing growth-intensive activities (Sobiech, 2019: 46).

One of the channels in which remittances affect the economic growth in a positive but indirect way shows itself in decreasing volatility (Arı & Özcan, 2011: 104). Remittances do not have too much volatility against economic activities such as FDI and direct portfolio investments, and they offer a stable source of funding. In addition, this stability helps a country to borrow at lower interest rates in international financial market by assuring the upcoming worker remittances (Gupta, Ptillio, & Wagh, 2007: 3). The fact that remittances are stable, reliable, and least volatile transfers has made them exist as crucial sources of national income for low-income countries specifically (Olaniyan, 2019: 20).

Sending countries are affected by not only the size but also the fluctuations of remittances. This is particularly the case of remittances coming from oil-rich Arab Gulf countries to the poor labor exporting Middle East countries. Remittances have been considered as a mechanism of redistributing oil revenue to those sending countries. This view doubts the positive impact of aid on development, so it is thought that remittances are more efficient than aid. The flows of workers and their remittances are sensitive to oil price shocks and political instability in the receiving countries, resulting in monumental movements of migrants, as happened during the oil price boosts between 1973 and 1979, and the oil price decreases in 1982 and 1986, as well as during Iraq's invasion to Kuwait (Glytsos, 2005: 470).

Remittances not only reduce poverty but also increase household savings and investments. For example, these transfers have not only been an important source of foreign exchange for Albania, but have also helped to finance the deficit stemming from trade goods and services since 1990. In fact, transfers have financed more than 70% of the current account deficit since 1995 (Mansoor & Quillin, 2007: 60–62). Although these transfers are seen as a source of investment for some countries, this may not be the case for others (Lucas, 2005: 152). For example, remittances sent by Turkish migrant workers who live and work in Germany could not be directed to investments, but were used to finance the foreign trade deficit. Therefore, it can be said that these transfers increase consumption rather than increasing the production in Turkey (Özyakışır, 2017: 1180). Although remittances have an ability to reduce poverty and sustain livelihoods for millions

of households, informality decreases tax revenues and undermines the rule of law. Sixty percent of the global workforce do not have formal job contracts, and this makes remittances somewhat controversial (Ivlevs, 2016: 1172).

From a negative perspective, remittances lead to Dutch disease effect, a labor supply contraction and a loss of external competitiveness. Moreover, remittance income would attract government in more corruption activity (Kratou & Gazdar, 2016: 52). Gupta et al. (2007) claim that the direct impact of remittances on growth depends on the use of received funds: on the effect of emigration on labor market supply and on country production.

Improving the official channels and developing the domestic financial sector can make remittance flow easier. This requires better quality, availability, and access of financial services to both senders and recipients. Developed financial sector products such as deposit and savings accounts, consumer loans, mortgages, insurance products, and pensions are also necessary. The participation of alternative financial institutions, namely community banks, savings, and private cooperatives, is important to enlarge access and outreach to low-income communities and unconnected rural areas that big commercial banks cannot reach. Governments, international organizations, and other related establishments can supply assistance to develop migrant households understanding and expertness to start small enterprises and thereby make the usage of remittances productive (Jha, Sugiyarto, & Vargas-Silva, 2010: 80).

3 Turkish Workers' Remittances

After two World Wars and the Great Depression, Europe entered into restructuring and industrialization. In this process, while capital accumulation and labor-intensive sectors are developing rapidly, the need for labor has emerged. In the same period, Turkey's demographic structure and labor surplus created by the current economic situation has triggered labor migration abroad since the 1960s. In this context, the numerical development of the workers sent abroad is given in Tab. 1 (Çan, 2010: 1).

The foreign exchange market was managed by the Central Bank of the Republic of Turkey (CBRT) in a very strict and controlled manner in the 1970s. During this period, the sell-off of the Turkish citizen was subject to permission. In 1976, for the first time, a foreign exchange deposit account was opened with the CBRT under the name of "Foreign Exchange Account with Credit Letters" for Turkish workers working abroad. The purpose of opening these accounts was to obtain more workers' remittances by the state. The biggest risk in this system was that banks had to transfer this currency to the CBRT. Also there was an

Tab. 1: Number of Turkish Migrant Workers Sent Abroad. Source: Çan, M. F. (2010). Gurbetçi dövizleri ve Türkiye, Fırat Kalkınma Ajansı, 1–7

Years	Number of Workers	Years	Number of Workers
1961	1.476	1971	88.444
1962	11.185	1972	85.229
1963	30.328	1973	135.820
1964	66.186	1974	20.211
1965	51.520	1975	4.419
1966	34.410	1976	10.558
1967	8.947	1977	19.084
1968	43.204	1978	18.582
1969	103.975	1979	23.630
1970	129.575	1980	28.503

exchange rate risk. This system continued in this way until the liberalization of capital movements in 1983 (Sarıtaş, 2011: 166–167).

Due to a military coup, remittance flows decreased in the early 1980s, but it stabilized in the second half of 1980s and rose gradually in the second half of 1990s, following the economic crisis in 1994. Interestingly, after a great earthquake disaster, remittances declined severely in 1999. It indicates the dominance of investment aim as the possible driving force of migrant remittances, rather than the motive of altruism (Karagöz, 2009: 1897). The economic and financial crises in November 2000 and February 2001 caused substantial declines in production and employment. The crisis erodes the confidence of the migrants to the economy causing them to remit through illegal channels or simply not remit at least for investment aims (Tansel & Yaşar, 2010: 5).

After the crisis in 2001, a severe decrease in the Turkish workers' remittance flow is seen. This may be an outcome of demographic change in sociological structure and entrepreneurial skills of emigrants. It is also possible that the third generation of Turkish migrants in Western Europe do not think to remit their earnings. Besides, entrepreneurship becomes more common in recent years among Western European Turkish migrants. This trend lowers the remittances during the second half of 2000s and first half of 2010s (Karagöz, 2009: 1897) (Fig. 4).

In the literature of finance in Turkey, there are few studies about the relationship between remittances and financial development (Ege & Şahin, 2014: 11). In one of these studies, Sayan (2004: 68) stressed the importance of workers' remittances for Turkey's economy; and he examined the relationship between Turkish migrants' remittances and economic fluctuations in Turkey and

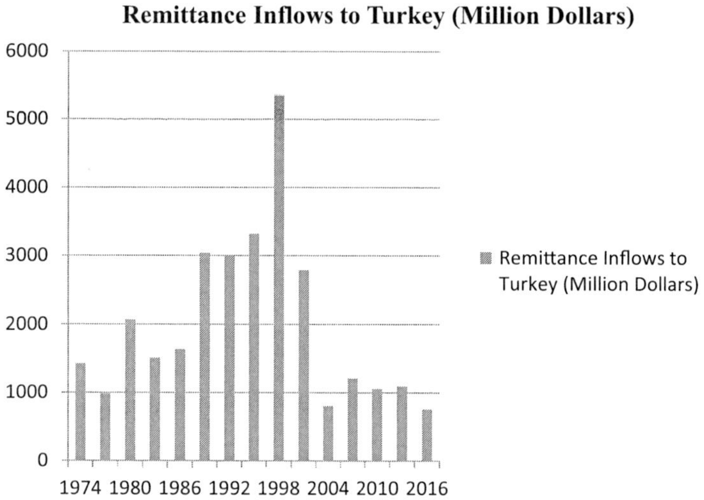

Fig. 4: Remittance Inflows to Turkey. Source: World Bank, Remittance Inflows to GDP for Turkey [DDOI11TRA156NWDB], retrieved from FRED, Federal Reserve Bank of St. Louis; https://fred.stlouisfed.org/series/DDOI11TRA156NWDB, June 26, 2019

Germany. He found that inward remittances to Turkey were not affected by fluctuations in German economy, but they were sensitive to changes in Turkey's economy. Ağır, Kar, and Nazlıoğlu (2011: 454), as a result of panel data analysis conducted on MENA countries including Turkey, found that remittances have positive effects on financial development.

Aydaş, Özcan, and Neyaptı (2005: 65) investigated the determining factors of Turkish workers' remittances. They found that the black market premium, interest rate differential, inflation rate, both home and host countries' incomes, and the period of military regime have significantly affected remittance flows in Turkey. They conclude that macroeconomic variables impact on inward remittances to Turkey, indicating that governments of labor-exporting countries can influence the inflow of remittances by means of appropriate macroeconomic policies. They also imply that improving financial intermediation and preventing exchange rate misalignments help escalating the inflow of remittances to Turkey.

Conclusion

Migration movements gained momentum with the globalization process and took on a global character. Migrants' remittances, which increased with the

phenomenon of global migration, have reached the dimensions that will contribute to the family economies in the past and now to the national economies. These remittances may exceed FDI and official foreign aid in some countries.

Migrant remittances, which are more stable than other financial sources, became a primary source of foreign exchange for supporting economic growth of developing countries by financing the current account deficit, reducing poverty, increasing consumption expenditures, and increasing household savings and investments.

Like financial sector development, migrants' transfers may contribute positively to economic growth when such transfers are used productively by migrants' families, rather than for unproductive consumption purposes. At this point, it can be said that Turkish migrants' remittances are mainly used for consumption instead of investment.

When compared with the previous years, it is seen that there is a significant decrease in the amount of foreign exchange in the Central Bank of the Republic of Turkey, and that the investment made by Turkish migrants who live abroad (especially in the local area) do not create any added-value and employment. On the contrary, it is observed that in the countries where Turkish migrants live, they developed their existing investments and their investments have increased numerically. This can be interpreted as the missing of a great opportunity for Turkey and the Turkish economy.

By establishing appropriate methods and grounds, the remittances of Turkish migrants should be drawn to Turkey, especially to the regions where there is a lack of capital and employment problem. In this regard, large duties fall to public and private sector (especially financial sector), development agencies, nongovernmental organizations, and even Turkish migrant workers who have ties with Turkey.

In summary, it can be asserted that Turkish finance literature supports complementarity hypothesis. Remittances and financial development support each other in promoting economic growth; and migrants can send money to their home countries cheaply, safely, and faster when there is a highly developed financial sector. As the financial sector in Turkey develops, it can expect a stable rise in remittances. If these remittances are used for investment rather than consumption, it can be a bigger effect on Turkey's economic growth.

Bibliography

Ağır, H., Kar, M., & Nazlıoğlu, Ş. (2011). Do remittances matter for financial development in the MENA region: Panel cointegration and causality analysis. *Empirical Economics Letters, 10*(5), 449–456.

Akçay, S. (2018). Remittances and misery index in Turkey: Is there a link? *Applied Economics Letters, 25*(13), 895–899.

Arı, A., & Özcan, B. (2011). İşçi gelirleri ve ekonomik büyüme ilişkisi: Dinamik panel veri analizi. *Erciyes Üniversitesi İktisadi ve İdari Bilimler Fakültesi Dergisi, 38*, 101–117.

Aydas, O. T., Özcan, K. M., & Neyaptı, B. (2005). Determinants of workers' remittances: The case of Turkey, *Emerging Markets Finance and Trade, 41*(3), 53–69.

Azam, M., & Khan, A. (2011). Workers' remittances and economic growth: Evidence from Azerbaijan and Armenia. *Global Journal of Human Social Science Research, 11*(7), 40–46.

Borjas, J. G. (1994). The economics of immigration. *Journal of Economic Literature, 32*, 1667–1717.

Boubtane, E., Dumont, J., & Rault, C. (2014). Immigration and economic growth in the OECD countries, 1986–2006 (IZA Discussion Paper No. 8681, pp. 1–33).

Çan, M. F. (2010). Gurbetçi dövizleri ve Türkiye. *Fırat Kalkınma Ajansı*, 1–7.

Ege, İ., & Şahin, S. (2014). Doğrudan yabancı sermaye yatırımı, işçi dövizleri ve bankacılık sektörü gelişimi: Türkiye örneği. *Finans Politik ve Ekonomik Yorumlar, 51*(598), 9–17.

Eggoh, J., Bangake, C., & Semedo, G. (2019). Do remittances spur economic growth? Evidence from developing countries. *The Journal of International Trade & Economic Development, 28*(4), 391–418.

Giuliano, P., & Arranz, L. (2009). Remittances, financial development and growth. *Journal of Development Economics, 90*(1), 144–152.

Glytsos, N. P. (2005). The contribution of remittances to growth: A dynamic approach and empirical analysis. *Journal of Economic Studies, 32*(6), 468–496.

Gupta, M. R., & Chakraborty, B. (2006). Human Capital Accumulation and Endogenous Growth in a Dual Economy. Hitotsubashi Journal of Economics, 47(2), 169–195.

Gupta, S., Ptillio, C., & Wagh, S. (2007). L'impact bénéfique des envois de fonds sur l'Afrique. *Finances & Développement, 44*(2), 40–43.

https://www.statista.com/statistics/268173/countries-with-the-largest-gross-domestic-product-gdp/ (Retrieved on 01.07.2019).

Ivlevs, A. (2016). Remittances and informal work. *International Journal of Manpower, 37*(7), 1172–1190.

Jha, S., Sugiyarto, S., & Vargas-Silva, C. (2010). The global crisis and the impact on remittances to developing Asia. *Global Economic Review, 39*(1), 59–82.

Karagöz, K. (2009). Workers' remittances and economic growth: Evidence from Turkey. *Journal of Yaşar University*, *4*(13), 1891–1908.

KNOMAD. (2017). *Migration and remittances: Recent developments and outlook*, April 2017.

Kratou, H., & Gazdar, K. (2016). Adressing the effect of workers' remittance on economic growth: Evidence from MENA countries. *International Journal of Social Economics*, *43*(1), 51–70.

Laczko, F. (2005). Migration, development and poverty in Asia. In *Migration, development and poverty reduction in Asia*. Geneva: International Organization for Migration.

Lucas, R. E. B. (2005). *International migration regimes and economic development*. Cheltenham, UK: Edward Elgar.

Mansoor, A., & Quillin, B. (2007). *Migration and remittances: Eastern Europe and the former Soviet Union*. Washington, DC: World Bank.

Mundaca, G. (2009). Remittances, financial market development, economic growth: The case of Latin America and the Caribbean. *Review of Development Economics*, *13*(2), 288–303.

Olaniyan, T. O. (2019). Interactive effects of remittances and financial sector development on economic growth in Nigeria. *Remittances Review*, *4*(1), 19–39.

Özyakışır, D. (2017). Ekonomik kalkınmada göçmen transferlerinin rolü: Mit mi gerçek mi? *İnsan ve Toplum Bilimleri Araştırmaları Dergisi*, *6*(2), 1172–1188.

Sarıtaş, H. (2011). İşçi dövizlerinin Türkiye Merkez Bankası bilançosuna etkisi. *Uluslararası Alanya İşletme Fakültesi Dergisi*, *3*(1), 163–182.

Sayan, S. (2004). Guest workers remittances and output fluctuations in host and home countries: The case of remittances from Turkish workers. *Emerging Markets Finance and Trade*, *40*(6), 68–81.

Sobiech, I. (2019). Remittances, finance and growth: Does financial development foster the impact of remittances on economic growth? *World Development*, *113*, 44–59.

Tansel, A., & Yaşar, P. (2010). *Macroeconomic impact of remittances on output growth: Evidence from Turkey* (Iza Discussion Paper, No. 5376, December 2010).

Vargas-Lundiu, R., Lanly, G., Villareal, M., & Osorio, M. (2008). *International migration, remittances and rural development*. Rome: International Fund for Agricultural Development (IFAD) Italy Publication.

World Bank. Remittance Inflows to GDP for Turkey [DDOI11TRA156NWDB]. Retrieved from FRED, Federal Reserve Bank of St. Louis. https://fred.stlouisfed.org/series/DDOI11TRA156NWDB, June 26, 2019.

Zhang, X., & Lin, S. (2010). The impact of the global slowdown on the People's Republic of China's rural migrants: Empirical evidence from a 12-city survey. In A. Bauer & M. Thant (Eds.), *Poverty and sustainable development in Asia: Impacts and responses to the global economic crisis* (pp. 203–218). Mandaluyong City: Asian Development Bank.

Ümit Yıldız and Bülent Günsoy

Chapter Four: Credit Ratings, Credit Rating Agencies, and Sovereign Credit Ratings[1]

Abstract: Especially in the last century, globalization and deregulation have shown intensively in every field with technological advances. These developments have affected the financial markets as well as in all other areas of the economic system, and restrictions and obstacles between countries have started to lose their effect rapidly. At this point, however, a crucial need arose for market participants: accurate information. For market participants who want to know about the risk they take when making an investment decision, accessing the accurate information is costly; and this negatively affects market discipline. At this point, credit rating is the most important tool to ensure market discipline.Credit rating is briefly defined as an independent assessment on whether an obligator can fulfill its financial obligations on time. This assestment is carried out by credit rating agencies within the framework of a certain method. Although there are many local and national rating agencies around the world, there are big three credit rating agencies (CRAs) which hold almost the entire market: Standard and Poor's (S&P), Fitch, and Moody's.Credit rating can be classified into many different subcategories. The rating can be classified as long- or short-term ratings according to their maturities, and local currency and foreign currency ratings according to their types. After risk assessment in the light of some economic and political factors for a country, the alpha numerical indicators determined in terms of long-term foreign currency are called Sovereign Credit Rating. Sovereign Credit Ratings are determined and announced by the CRAs. CRAs determine sovereign credit ratings on a scale that consists of many levels ranging from 'prime' level to 'default' level. This scale also shows the rating grades of the agencies. The scale used by CRAs is classified into three different levels: investment grade, non-investment grade, and default grade.

Keywords: Credit rating, credit rating agencies, sovereign credit ratings, Standard & Poor's, Fitch, Moody's

Introduction

The world has been undergoing rapid change and development for centuries. This change, which continues to be experienced in every aspect of life, has gained momentum especially in the last century and has caused new phenomena and new needs in many areas. In addition, the technological advances experienced in

1 This study is based on a Master's Thesis titled "Credit Rating Agencies and Macroeconomics Determinants of Sovereign Credit Ratings: Panel Data Analysis."

this period have been effective in almost every field. Phenomena such as globalization, deregulation, and liberalization, which have developed in parallel with technological advances, have had their effects on all economies in the world and caused almost all economic policies to be shaped within this framework.

These developments, which significantly affect economic decision-making processes, have also affected financial markets and made financial markets a global market. Together with the decrease in the restrictions between economies, significant developments have been experienced in financial investments as well as direct capital investments; and this has enabled the investors to move freely in the whole market.

These recent developments have created a number of requirements for market participants to make the right decision. In other words, this development led to the necessity of having the available information in order for the market participants to determine the risks they will face when making an investment decision. As a result, all of these revealed the need for credit rating.

Rating is briefly defined as an opinion that shows the risk of an institution to fulfill its obligations in a timely and complete manner. After the rating process, the determined creditworthiness of the obligor is announced with symbols consisting of a number of letters and numbers that are universal and easy to understand. There are many CRAs around the world. However, the top three organizations that represent a significant part of the industry are S&P's, Moody's, and Fitch. These big three organizations, recognized by investors worldwide, have the high impact on market and market participants' decisions. Of the three global players that dominate the credit rating business, Fitch's share is 15% of the market, while S&P and Moody's share is about 80% (Alsakka & Gwilym, 2010: 2615).

Although these CRAs provide credit ratings for many different financial instruments, the credit ratings determined especially for countries are closely monitored by investors. The credit ratings given to the countries are presented as short- and long-term ratings. At the same time this rating can be made in local currency or foreign currency. Within this framework, after risk assessment in the light of some economic and political factors, the alpha numerical results announced by the CRAs in terms of long-term foreign currency are called Sovereign Credit Rating. In this study, big three CRAs and sovereign credit ratings determined by these institutions are emphasized.

1 Definition of Credit Rating

Credit rating is briefly defined as an assessment of the creditworthiness of an obligor as an entity or with respect to specific securities, financial instruments,

and debt obligations (Schroeter, 2013: 379). According to a different definition, credit rating is an independent opinion on whether an institution can fulfill its financial obligations on time. In order for this view to be easily understood, the results are transformed into symbols with universal application (Berker, 2003: 2).

Credit rating is the assessment made to determine whether the issuer of the debt instrument will make the principal and interest payments of the debt on time (Karluk, 2009: 429). The rating that we define in this way can be classified into many different subcategories. At this point, the rating can be classified as long-term or short-term ratings according to their maturities and local currency and foreign currency ratings according to their types (Babuşcu, 2005: 105).

Long-term rating is the opinion given on the basis of the performance of the institution and the basic economic and financial characteristics of the sector to which the institution belongs and shows the likelihood of the fulfillment of obligations in the long term. On the other hand, short-term rating is the evaluation of access to liquidity and capital resources to meet liabilities up to one year. Ratings by type are divided into two as foreign currency or local currency ratings and assess the capacity to pay the liabilities in that currency by creating the relevant currency (Berker, 2003).

Şirvan (2004: 5) examines the rating under four headings according to the groups: sovereign rating, corporate rating, export rating, and project rating. Sovereign rating, which is among the mentioned types of ratings, can be defined as the process of measuring the willingness and capacity of a country to be able to meet its obligations in full and on time.

Another rating criterion is the rating according to the rating agency. Here we can examine credit rating under two headings: internal rating and external rating. Internal rating is the grade given by the banks to the borrowers according to their internal evaluation criteria (Yazıcı, 2009: 3). For internal rating, banks calculate the risk weights of their assets internally by certain measures based on risk weight function (Ankara Chamber of Commerce, 2007: 26). External rating is defined as an indicator credit rating made by rating agencies in order to enable relatively larger firms to borrow from capital markets (Yazıcı, 2009: 3).

After sorting the types of ratings in this way, we can expand the scope of the rating process. Credit rating is not limited to measuring the credibility of the rated institution, organization, country, or security. In addition to showing the capacity of institutions to fulfill their obligations in a timely manner, the credit rating also includes the process of mathematical expression of the risk taken when allocating loans to an enterprise or individual (Yaslıdağ, 2007: 129). Similarly, rating activities include studies to measure the risk factors that are

subject to rating using historical data within the framework of a given model (Yaslıdağ, 2007: 129).

Another important point to be mentioned is that the institution risks measured by CRAs are not evaluated independently from the sovereign risks of the countries in which they are located. Therefore, the credit ratings of the institutions are limited to the sovereign credit ratings. In this case, the fulfillment of liabilities, especially in foreign currencies, may become impossible if governments impose restrictions on foreign exchange transfers. Therefore, the sovereign rating is the limit for foreign currency rating. Therefore, in countries have a credit rating below investment grade, such as Turkey, it is difficult to make relative evaluation between institutions (Berker, 2003: 3).

1.1 Importance of Credit Ratings for Investors and Countries

Especially in the last century, globalization and deregulation have shown itself intensively in every field with technological advances and continue to show rapidly. These developments have affected the financial markets as well as in all other areas of the economic system, and restrictions and obstacles between countries have started to lose their effect rapidly. This has resulted in, except in some special cases, the free movement of financial capital in the world, just like the free movement of people, goods, and services. As a result, financial market participants began to move freely in financial markets. At this point, however, a crucial need arose for market participants: the accurate information. Because, market participants can make investment decisions only when they have effective and accurate information. However, for market participants who want to know about the risk they take when making an investment decision, accessing the accurate information is costly; and this negatively affects market discipline. At this point, rating is the most important tool to ensure market discipline. With this feature, rating provides the greatest service to individual investors who have limited access to information since it reaches to large masses (Berker, 2003: 2).

One of the most significant features of the rating process is the universal indicators used to announce the credit quality of the asset subject to the rating. Rating consists of powerful and useful symbols that help institutions, lenders and borrowers, investors, all intermediaries, and regulators to evaluate in the money markets and capital markets (Yazıcı, 2009: 3). CRAs that rate financial institutions, banks, and countries provide information to the investor by converting the data obtained as a result of the rating process into easy to understand and short symbols (Yaslıdağ, 2007: 130).

One of the most important points that we should emphasize for the rating process is that the rating should be carried out in appropriate conditions and

with the correct methods, and the announced credit ratings should be reliable and accurate. In this sense, financial institutions are required to allocate high provision for high risk assets in accordance with the banking regulations that they are obliged to comply with within the framework of Basel II and Basel III criteria. And especially the high dependence of the recently developed liquidity regulations on credit ratings has led financial markets to attach greater importance to the accuracy of credit ratings (Gür & Öztürk, 2011: 71).

Another important function of the rating process is the effect of the ratings on the market participants and the creditworthiness of the rated securities. Although it is stated that the rating made by the rating agencies is not an advice, the rating category has significant effects on the marketability of debt securities (Özdinç, 1999: 9).

The main function of the rating activity for the investor is to provide a ranking of the probability of payment by comparing rated and unrated securities (Acar Boyacıoğlu, 2005: 68). In addition, the rating, through easily understandable symbols, provides information to investors and fund holders about the quality and risk of securities issued and provides information to creditors about the repayment of credits issued (Yaslıdağ, 2007: 129).

Crises, which are increasingly encountered in the financial markets, are intensely due to the lack of regional and financial infrastructure. Therefore, the not repayment of the credits issued or the high risks in this regard impede the healthy functioning of financial markets and create important problems that lead the crisis. At this point, every market participant should be aware of the risk it takes for the markets to function properly (Berker, 2003). With this feature, credit rating provides convenience to market participants for assessing the risks of financial assets and making decisions.

Although credit rating is a subjective opinion, the ratings may affect investors' decisions. At the same time, financial resources related to investments such as doing business by local investors, borrowing from abroad, buying and selling bonds, and financing large infrastructure projects requiring external financing are all affected by the ratings given by these institutions (Karagöl, 2013: 8). The major source of financing for large-scale investments in the financial markets is government bonds. Government bonds, which account for more than 40% of the globally issued bond stocks, are now an important investment option in the hands of investors. For this reason, the existence of globally accepted and consistent credit rating criteria that can help investors in their investment decisions is very important (Dimitrijevic, 2012: 2).

On the other hand, although the purchase of the securities depends on the investor's attitude about risk, it is observed that the investors generally turn to

the lower-risk securities. However, this does not mean that high-risk securities cannot be marketed. If the risk is compensated, the possibility of marketing high-risk securities increases (Özdinç, 1999: 9–10).

In financial markets, credit ratings are important for lenders as well as for borrowers to eliminate serious risks. Borrowers, that is, the issuers of any debt instrument, should also be aware of the risk it takes. In this respect, the rating also includes the necessary financial evaluation for borrowers (Berker, 2003).

With the liberalization of financial markets, international funds have started to move freely in international financial markets. However, which financial asset, which institution, or which country will these funds be directed to? Today, one of the various economic and political factors that determine which countries the international fund will turn to is the ratings given by CRAs to measure sovereign risk (Erdoğan & Ener, 2000: 30). In addition to many criteria, investors also take decisions based on credit ratings given by rating agencies. In this case, the demand for bonds or bills of countries which have high credit ratings is higher than those countries which have low credit ratings. Investors prefer low risk and turn to bonds of low-risk countries. With this feature, the credit ratings are used by investors, borrowers, creditors, and governments and play an important role in the financial markets (Commission of the European Communities, 2008: 2).

An important point to note when mentioning the importance of rating for countries is related to developing countries. While developing countries finance their development, they need international funds due to insufficiencies in their own resources. Accurate determination of the credibility of borrowing institutions is of great importance in the international markets in which countries, public institutions, private sector organizations, financial institutions, and investors come together. Therefore, credit ratings have become a more widely used indicator in regulation and risk management process (Gür & Öztürk, 2011: 71).

The fact that credit ratings contain explanatory information about country risk undoubtedly affects the economies of the country to a great extent. The effects of ratings on the country's economy and markets are summarized as follows (Yazıcı, 2009: 4):

- Rating builds confidence in the economy and brings stability in developing financial markets
- Rating ensures integration of markets with international markets
- Rating limits the overall risk level in the economy and increases the efficiency of financial transactions.

2 Credit Rating Agencies

Credit rating with the shortest and clearest definition means assessment of the capacity of the debtor to pay the principal and interest on time and in full. This assessment is carried out by CRAs within the framework of a certain method. Although there are many local and national rating agencies around the world, the study focuses on S&P's, Fitch, and Moody's, which hold almost the entire market.

When examining the types of ratings, we mentioned that the rating is classified into subcategories according to maturity, currency, rating agency, and rated asset. In this part of the study, the sovereign ratings among the mentioned types are emphasized and the long-term foreign currency ratings determined by these big three international CRAs are examined.

Most commonly, CRAs are defined as independent credibility viewers, whose ratings are used by governments, investors, securities issuers, and debtors for various reasons (ESME, 2008: 3). These organizations have emerged as a result of the need for information providers to act as intermediaries in accessing the information they need in order to make investment decisions of market participations in capital markets. Rating agencies are intermediaries that eliminate the lack of information of investors and other market participants in financial markets and have an important responsibility for the efficient functioning of the markets. Rating is a tool that guides market players and allows market participants to evaluate their investments in the risk group they deem appropriate.

CRAs present independent opinions on the probability of default or expected losses of companies, governments, and a wide range of financial instruments (EU Commission, 2008: 2). In addition, these institutions, by measuring the risks of repayment, inform investors who want to make financial investment by buying treasury bills or bonds (Karluk, 2009: 429). For this reason, many market actors who are in need of borrowing in financial markets or who want to invest in securities closely monitor the activities of CRAs. Rating agencies use certain categories in their ratings regarding debt securities and show the categories with easily understandable symbols consisting of letters, numbers, or a mixture of these (Özdinç, 1999: 8). These symbols set an international standard for easy understanding of the risks of the asset subject to the rating.

The rapid development of the rating sector and the incorporation of many organizations into the sector have led to developments that disrupt the healthy functioning of the market. In 1975, U.S. Securities and Exchange Commission (SEC) established National Recognized Statistical Rating Organization (NRSRO) to bring a standard to the activities of rating agencies and gathered rating agencies

under a single roof. The institution, which initially had three members, now has 10 members (Yazıcı, 2009: 6).

The agencies that are members of NRSRO can be listed as follows:[2]

- *S&P's Ratings Services*
- *Moody's Investor Service*
- *Fitch Ratings*
- *Japan Credit Rating Agency*
- *Morningstar Credit Ratings*
- *A.M. Best Company*
- *Kroll Bond Rating Agency*
- *DBRS*
- *HR Ratings de Mexico*
- *Egan-Jones Ratings Company*

2.1 Functions and Importance of Credit Rating Agencies in Financial Markets

Financial markets are rapidly adapting to the rapidly developing world and are in parallel with all global changes. And as in all other areas, capital markets have become a structure without borders. However, in order for this system to function properly, it was quite difficult to obtain the necessary information, and a system was needed to bridge this gap. At this point, international CRAs emerged to fill the lack of information between investors and institutions (Birdişli, 2012: 445). In its most clear explanation, the aim of CRAs is to eliminate the problem of asymmetric information between borrowers and lenders in financial markets (Kanlı & Barlas, 2011: 1). These organizations, established to eliminate or at least minimize the asymmetric information problem in the market, have also undertaken the task of regulating and supervising the financial markets. Therefore, the ratings given by rating agencies are used as a criterion in the regulation and supervision of financial markets and are the basis for determining the risk weights in international or local regulations such as Basel II criteria (Yazıcı, 2009).

Despite all the negative developments in recent years, sovereign credit ratings determined by CRAs continue to be important indicators for investors. Credit ratings are effective in the formation of risk perceptions of individual or institutional investors towards countries. Investors' risk perceptions have important implications

2 https://www.sec.gov/2018-annual-report-on-nrsros.pdf (Date accessed, 01.08.2019).

for monetary and fiscal policies in national economies (Acar, 2011: 10–11). It is both time consuming and costly to investigate the economic and political structure of the countries for each investor or lender in international markets. CRAs with expert economists can access information in a much shorter time than any investor (Erdoğan & Ener, 2000: 33).

2.2 The Three Major Credit Rating Agencies

There are many national, regional, or international rating agencies around the world. However, S&P's, Moody's, and Fitch are the big three CRAs among these agencies (Yazıcı, 2009: 6).

2.2.1 Standard and Poor's

S&P, founded in 1860 with the publication of the *History of Railroads and Canals in the USA* written by economics analyst Henry Varnum Poor, publishes credit ratings since 1916 and provides independent credit risk analyses for investors and market participants worldwide (S&P, Guide of Credit Rating Essentials, 2011). S&P, whose roots date back 150 years, has more than 1,500 analysts, managers, and economists in its offices worldwide.[3] Explanations on S&P Long-Term Credit Ratings are given in Tab. 1.

2.2.2 Fitch Ratings

As one of the three major CRAs, Fitch determines sovereign credit rating in short- and long-term and in local and foreign currencies similar to other CRAs. Table 2 presents explanations of the Fitch's long-term foreign currency credit ratings. As can be seen from the table, Fitch and S&P use the same grade scale.

2.2.3 Moody's Investors Service

Moody's Investors Service, whose parent company is Moody's Corporation[4], is one of the three leading agencies in the rating industry, working on credit ratings and risk analyses. The firm's ratings and analysis track debt covering more than 135 sovereign nations, approximately 4,800 nonfinancial corporate issuers, 4,100 financial institutions issuers, 17,600 public finance issuers, 9,600 structured finance transactions, and 1,000 infrastructure and project finance issuers.[5]

---

3 https://www.spglobal.com/ratings/en/about/index.aspx (Date accessed: 01.08.2019).
4 Moody's Corporation is the parent company of Moody's Investors Service and Moody's Analytics.
5 https://www.moodys.com/Pages/atc.aspx (Date accessed: 01.08.2019).

Tab. 1: S&P's Long-Term Credit Ratings. Source: S&P https://www.standardandpoors.com/en_AP/web/guest/article/-/view/sourceId/504352 Date accessed: 01.08.2019

Rating	Explanation
AAA	An obligation rated 'AAA' has the highest rating assigned by S&P Global Rating. The obligor's capacity to meet its financial commitments on the obligation is extremely strong.
AA	An obligation rated 'AA' differs from highest-rated obligations by only a small degree. The obligor's capacity to meet its financial commitments on the obligation is very strong.
A	An obligation rated 'A' is somewhat more susceptible to the adverse effects of changes in circumstances and economic conditions than obligations in higher-rated categories. However, the obligor's capacity to meet its financial commitments on the obligation is still strong.
BBB	An obligation rated 'BBB' exhibits adequate protection parameters. However, adverse economic conditions or changing circumstances are more likely to weaken the obligor's capacity to meet its financial commitments on the obligation.
BB	An obligation rated 'BB' is less vulnerable to nonpayment than other speculative issues. However, it faces major ongoing uncertainties or exposure to adverse business, financial, or economic conditions that could lead to the obligor's inadequate capacity to meet its financial commitments on the obligation.
B	An obligation rated 'B' is more vulnerable to nonpayment than obligations rated 'BB', but the obligor currently has the capacity to meet its financial commitments on the obligation. Adverse business, financial, or economic conditions will likely impair the obligor's capacity or willingness to meet its financial commitments on the obligation.
CCC	An obligation rated 'CCC' is currently vulnerable to nonpayment and is dependent upon favorable business, financial, and economic conditions for the obligor to meet its financial commitments on the obligation. In the event of adverse business, financial, or economic conditions, the obligor is not likely to have the capacity to meet its financial commitments on the obligation.
CC	An obligation rated 'CC' is currently highly vulnerable to nonpayment. The 'CC' rating is used when a default has not yet occurred but S&P Global Ratings expects default to be a virtual certainty, regardless of the anticipated time to default.
C	An obligation rated 'C' is currently highly vulnerable to nonpayment, and the obligation is expected to have lower relative seniority or lower ultimate recovery compared with obligations that are rated higher.
D	An obligation rated 'D' is in default or in breach of an imputed promise.

Tab. 2: Fitch's Long-Term Credit Ratings. Source: Fitch Ratings, https://www.fitchratings.com/site/dam/jcr:6b03c4cd-611d-47ec-b8f1-183c01b51b08/Rating Date accessed: 01.08.2019

Rating	Definition	Explanation
AAA	Highest credit quality	'AAA' ratings denote the lowest expectation of default risk. They are assigned only in cases of exceptionally strong capacity for payment of financial commitments. This capacity is highly unlikely to be adversely affected by foreseeable events.
AA	Very high credit quality	'AA' ratings denote expectations of very low default risk. They indicate very strong capacity for payment of financial commitments. This capacity is not significantly vulnerable to foreseeable events.
A	High credit quality	'A' ratings denote expectations of low default risk. The capacity for payment of financial commitments is considered strong. This capacity may, nevertheless, be more vulnerable to adverse business or economic conditions than is the case for higher ratings.
BBB	Good credit quality	'BBB' ratings indicate that expectations of default risk are currently low. The capacity for payment of financial commitments is considered adequate, but adverse business or economic conditions are more likely to impair this capacity.
BB	Speculative	'BB' ratings indicate an elevated vulnerability to default risk, particularly in the event of adverse changes in business or economic conditions over time; however, business or financial flexibility exists that supports the servicing of financial commitments.
B	Highly speculative	'B' ratings indicate that material default risk is present, but a limited margin of safety remains. Financial commitments are currently being met; however, capacity for continued payment is vulnerable to deterioration in the business and economic environment.
CCC	Substantial credit risk	Default is a real possibility.
CC	Very high levels of credit risk	Default of some kind appears probable.
C	Near default	A default or default-like process has begun, or the issuer is in standstill, or for a closed funding vehicle, payment capacity is irrevocably impaired.
D	Default	'D' ratings indicate an issuer that in Fitch's opinion has entered into bankruptcy filings, administration, receivership, liquidation, or other formal winding-up procedure or that has otherwise ceased business.

Tab. 3: Moody's Long-Term Credit Ratings. Source: Moody's Investor Service, https://www.moodys.com/ratings-process/Ratings-Definitions/002002 Date accessed: 01.08.2019

Rating	Explanation
Aaa	Obligations rated 'Aaa' are judged to be of the highest quality, subject to the lowest level of credit risk.
Aa	Obligations rated 'Aa' are judged to be of high quality and are subject to very low credit risk.
A	Obligations rated 'A' are judged to be upper-medium grade and are subject to low credit risk.
Baa	Obligations rated 'Baa' are judged to be medium-grade and subject to moderate credit risk and as such may possess certain speculative characteristics.
Ba	Obligations rated 'Ba' are judged to be speculative and are subject to substantial credit risk.
B	Obligations rated 'B' are considered speculative and are subject to high credit risk.
Caa	Obligations rated 'Caa' are judged to be speculative of poor standing and are subject to very high credit risk.
Ca	Obligations rated 'Ca' are highly speculative and are likely in, or very near, default, with some prospect of recovery of principal and interest.
C	Obligations rated 'C' are the lowest rated and are typically in default, with little prospect for recovery of principal or interest.

Like other CRAs, Moody's assesses the credit risks of many countries, institutions, or securities and determines a credit rating for these assets. However, in this section, as in the other headings, only the explanations of long-term credit ratings are given and long-term foreign currency credit ratings are emphasized. Table 3 presents explanations of the Moody's long-term foreign currency credit ratings.

3 Sovereign Credit Ratings

According to Afonso, Gomes, and Rother (2007: 5), sovereign credit ratings are a condensed assessment of a government's ability and willingness to repay its public debt both in principal and in interests on time. With this feature, the sovereign credit rating is one of the most important universal indicators showing the creditworthiness of a country. Sovereign credit ratings representing country risk are determined and announced by national or international independent organizations called CRAs. Sovereign credit ratings determined by the CRAs

are accepted as an indicator of the countries' capacity to fulfill their financial obligations (Kanlı & Barlas, 2011: 1).

Sovereign credit ratings can be determined in local currency or foreign currency. CRAs mainly focus on the country's economic and political indicators when determining a foreign currency sovereign credit rating. CRAs also take into account the resilience of countries to fluctuations in the markets when rating countries. If the country has strong internal dynamics, the local currency credit rating can be higher than the foreign currency credit rating (Çevik, 2011: 3).

The three major international CRAs that we focus on in our study have measured country risks for many years and have determined sovereign credit ratings for countries. For example, S&P has been providing sovereign credit ratings since 1961 and Moody's has been providing sovereign credit ratings since 1974 (Bissoondoyal-Bheenick, 2005: 254).

3.1 Importance of Sovereign Credit Ratings

Sovereign credit ratings are basically classified into two categories: investment grade and non-investment grade. The investment grade level serves as a threshold for countries' access to external financing. In this sense, the sovereign credit ratings at the investment and non-investment grade levels are considered as different risk groups in financial markets. In addition, some existing laws and regulations allow many long-term funds, such as pension and insurance funds, to be invested only in countries with a rating at investment grade. In other words, a credit rating at investment grade causes significant changes in the risk perception of the country and enables the country to have a wider potential investor base (Kanlı & Barlas, 2011). Otherwise, a speculative credit rating of the country causes a high risk perception of the country, and this results in the investor potential not being reached to the desired level.

3.2 Credit Rating Agencies' Rating Scales

CRAs determine credit ratings for both countries and companies on a scale that consists of many levels ranging from 'prime' level to 'default' level (Kanlı & Barlas, 2011: 3). This scale also shows the rating grades of the agencies. Table 4 lists the ratings given by S&P, Fitch, and Moody's from the lowest risk credit rating to the highest risk credit rating.

As can be seen from the table, the lowest risk level is 'AAA' for S&P and Fitch and 'Aaa' for Moody's. For both an institution and a country, this level means that the borrower is extremely strong in meeting its obligations and that there

Tab. 4: CRAs' Rating Scales. Source: S&P, Fitch, and Moody's

S&P's	Fitch's	Moody's	Definition
AAA	AAA	Aaa	Investment grade
AA+	AA+	Aa1	
AA	AA	Aa2	
AA-	AA-	Aa3	
A+	A+	A1	
A	A	A2	
A-	A-	A3	
BBB+	BBB+	Baa1	
BBB	BBB	Baa2	
BBB-	BBB-	Baa3	
BB+	BB+	Ba1	Non-investment grade
BB	BB	Ba2	
BB-	BB-	Ba3	
B+	B+	B1	
B	B	B2	
B-	B-	B3	
CCC+	CCC+	Caa1	
CCC	CCC	Caa2	
CCC-	CCC-	Caa3	
CC	CC	Ca	
D/SD	DDD/DD/D	C	Default

is almost no risk of fulfilling the obligations on time and in full. As it moves downward from each column of the table, the risk increases in this respect, and at some point it reaches the speculative level. The bottom column of the table shows the 'default' level in which there is no longer the possibility of fulfilling the obligations. In short, the scale used by CRAs is classified into three different levels: investment grade, non-investment (speculative) grade, and default grade.

The investment grade includes grades from AAA to BBB- for S&P and Fitch, while the investment grades for Moody's is from Aaa to Baa3. These grades are desirable for investors, institutions, countries, or any financial market participant, as it represents the lowest risk perception. On the other hand, at the non-investment grade, the risk perception of market players is increasing. At this grade, CC for S&P and Fitch, and Ca for Moody's are credit ratings where the risk is at the highest level; and the obligations are almost impossible to fulfill. Finally, D, DD, DDD, SD, and C represent the credit rating levels called as default.

Bibliography

Acar Boyacıoğlu, M. (2005). *Bankalarda derecelendirme (rating) ve Türk bankacılık sektörü üzerine amprik bir çalışma*. İstanbul: Ünal Aysal Tez Değerlendirme Yarışma Dizisi.

Acar, O. (2011). *Yapısal reformsuz kredi artışı olmaz*. TEPAV.

Afonso, A., Gomes, P., & Rother, P. (2007). *What hides behind sovereign debt ratings?* (European Central Bank Working Paper Series, No. 711).

Alsakka, R., & Gwilym, O. (2010). Leads and lags in soverign credit ratings. *Journal of Banking & Finance, 34*, 2614–2626

Ankara Chamber of Commerce. (2007). *Basel II kobilerin kredi riski ve derecelendirmesi*. Ankara: Yorum Basın Yayın.

Babuşcu, Ş. (2005). *Basel II düzenlemeleri çerçevesinde bankalarda risk yönetimi*. Ankara: Akademi Araştırma Planlama Danışmanlık Eğitim Yayıncılık.

Berker, A. B. (2003). Derecelendirme kuruluşları. http://www.fitchratings.com.tr/ftp/de recelendirme/drc_23.pdf (Date accessed: 10.01.2014).

Birdişli, F. (2012). Küresel ekonomik sistemin işleyişi içinde kredi derecelendirme kurumlarının işlevleri. http://iys.inonu.edu.tr/webpanel/dosyalar/1427/file/F_Bir disli.pdf (Date accessed: 10.01.2014).

Bissoondoyal-Bheenick, E. (2005). An analysis of the determinants of sovereign ratings. *Global Finance Journal, 15*, 251–280.

Çevik, B. (2011). Kredi notları ve CDS ilişkisi sona mı erdi? İşbankası İktisadi Araştırmalar Bölümü. http://ekonomi.isbank.com.tr/UserFiles/pdf/ar_03_2011.pdf (Date accessed: 15.01.2014).

Dimitrijevic, A. (2012). Ülke kredi notunu nasıl belirliyoruz. http://www.standardandpoors.com/spf/upload/Ratings_EMEA/20120301_UlkerlerinKrediNotunuBasilBelirliyoruz.pdf (Date accessed: 11.01.2014).

Erdoğan, E., & Ener, M. (2000). Kredi derecelendirme kuruluşlarının küresel boyutlu finansal yönelimlerdeki rolü ve Türkiye değerlendirmesi. *İktisat, İşletme ve Finans Dergisi, 15*(168), 29–39.

ESME. (2008). Role of credit rating agencies. http://ec.europa.eu/internal_market/securities/docs/agencies/report_040608_en.pdf (Date accessed: 10.01.2014).

Commission of The European Communities. (2008). *Regulation of the European Parliament and of the Council on credit rating agencies* (No. 0217).

Gür, T. H., & Öztürk, H. (2011). Ülke riski, derecelendirme kuruluşlar, aksaklıklar ve yeni düzenlemeler. *Sosyoekonomi Dergisi, 2*, 69–92.

Kanlı, İ. B., & Barlas, Y. (2011). *Eşiği aşınca: kredi notunun 'yatırım yapılabilir' seviyeye yükselmesinin etkileri*. Ankara: TCMB.

Karagöl, E. T. (2013). Kredi derecelendirme kuruluşları. *Uzman Bakış Dergisi, 1*, 8–11.

Karluk, R. (2009). *Cumhuriyetin ilanından günümüze Türkiye Ekonomisi'nde yapısal dönüşüm*. İstanbul: Beta Yayıncılık.

Özdinç, Ö. (1999). *Derecelendirme sürecinde ekonometrik bir değerlendirme*. Ankara: Sermaye Piyasası Kurulu.

Standard & Poor's. (2011). *S&P, guide of credit rating essentials*. http://www.standardandpoors.com/ spf/upload/Ratings_EMEA/kredi_derecelendirmelerini_tanima_rehberi.pdf, Access Date: 01.02.2014.

Schroeter, U. G. (2013). *Handbook of key global financial markets, ınstitutions, and ınfrastructure* (pp. 379–390), UK: Elsevier Inc.

Şirvan, N. (2004). Kredi derecelendirme ve Türkiye Ekonomisi. http://kurumsalyonetimzirvesi.com/files/downloads/bilgi_merkezi/kurumsal_yonetim_endeksi/kredi_derecelendirme_ve_turkiye_ekonomisi_nesrin_sirvan.pdf (Date accessed: 25.01.2014).

Yaslıdağ, B. (2007). *Kredi derecelendirme sistemi*. İstanbul: Literatür Yayınları.

Yazıcı, M. (2009). Kredi derecelendirme kuruluşlarının önemi ve denetimi. http://www.finanskulup.org.tr/ (Date accessed: 12.01.2014).

https://www.sec.gov/2018-annual-report-on-nrsros.pdf (Date accessed: 01.08.2019).

https://www.spglobal.com/ratings/en/about/index.aspx (Date accessed: 01.08.2019).

https://www.fitchratings.com/site/dam/jcr:6b03c4cd-611d-47ec-b8f1-183c01b51b08/Rating (Date accessed: 01.08.2019).

https://www.moodys.com/ratings-process/Ratings-Definitions/002002 (Date accessed: 01.08.2019).

https://www.moodys.com/Pages/atc.aspx (Date accessed: 01.08.2019).

https://www.standardandpoors.com/en_AP/web/guest/article/-/view/sourceId/504352 (Date accessed: 01.08.2019).

Özgür Bayram Soylu

Chapter Five: Financialization and Income Inequality

Abstract: The importance of the financial sector has increased since the 1980s. Today, this development is called financialization. The role of financial institutions and agents has played an important part in increasing the debates of financialization since the 2008 crisis. The financialization process can be defined as the increasing importance of the financial sector, which has an impact on the distribution of wages and profits, undistributed profits, and financial gains such as dividends and interests. Income inequality remains one of the main problems of the modern world economy. Even though technological advances ensure economic growth and international mobility of production factors, income inequality remains a solution for policymakers. Financialization and income inequality is one of the most important transformations of developed economies in recent years. Several factors contributed to the intensification of global inequality. The most important feature of this process is the slowdown in wage increases and in some cases the decrease in real wages. A second factor contributing to increased inequality is the pressure of governments to reduce public sector spending on much-needed physical and social infrastructure, particularly roads, immunization, rural health clinics, agricultural extension, and education. Another source of increasing inequality and the resulting shortage of demand is the exchange between central banks within the policy framework. The aim of this study is to review and introduce the literature from various perspectives focusing on financialization and income inequality.

Keywords: Financialization, distribution, income inequality, political economy

Introduction

The increasing role of the financial sector has brought about the concept of financialization since the 1980s. Financialization became particularly popular after the 2008 global crisis. National and international effects of financialization are remarkable with the global crisis. The role of financial institutions and agents have played an important role in increasing the debates of financialization since the 2008 crisis. Similarly, income distribution has become increasingly unequal in most developing and developed countries since the 1980s. In recent years, increasing financial instability and income inequality have become common features of political economies in wealthy capitalist democracies embodied by revolts such as the 2008 financial crisis and the Greek debt crisis (Hyde et al.

2018). At this point, the process of financialization is seen as the main driving force of inequality (Assa, 2012; Kus, 2012; Van Arnum & Naples, 2013; Zalewski & Whalen, 2010).

Financialization is a process in which financial markets, financial institutions, and financial elites gain a greater impact on economic policy and economic outcomes. Palley (2007) concentrated the effects of financialization on macro and microeconomic levels under three main headings. First, to increase the importance of the financial sector compared to the real sector; second, to transfer revenues from the real sector to the financial sector; and third; to increase income inequality and contribute to wage stagnation. In this context, financialization operates through three different channels: changes in the structure and operation of financial markets, changes in the behavior of nonfinancial companies, and changes in economic policy.

Although there has been some improvement in the global economy in terms of the decrease in the number of people living in absolute poverty in the last thirty years, inequality has increased within and between countries (Stiglitz, 2012). Labor-capital relations are changing in the era of financial capitalism. The share of labor and capital shifted to property incomes while wages were stagnant. The most important factors confirming the remarkable achievement of income inequality are financialization, labor flexibility, weakening of trade unions and withdrawal of the welfare state, transfers, and tax policies in the last 20 years (Pasquale Tridico).

The concept of financialization and the relationship between income inequality are theoretically discussed in this study. Section 1 provides an overview of financialization, and Section 2 provides and discusses the existing approaches to financialization. Section 3 examines the relationship between financialization and income inequality. The last section presents the conclusion.

1 The Concept of Financialization

The concept of financialization has been evaluated by many economists on different bases. The definitions of financialization are expressed in the context of real production, the role of the government in the economy, the income injustice, the role of financial intermediaries and institutions, and the expansion of financial capital.

Financialization is a term used to summarize a broad set of changes in the relationship between "financial" and "real" sectors, which have so far weighed more on financial actors or objectives (Stockhammer, 2010). The most common definition of financialization is the one expressed by Epstein (2005). Financialization

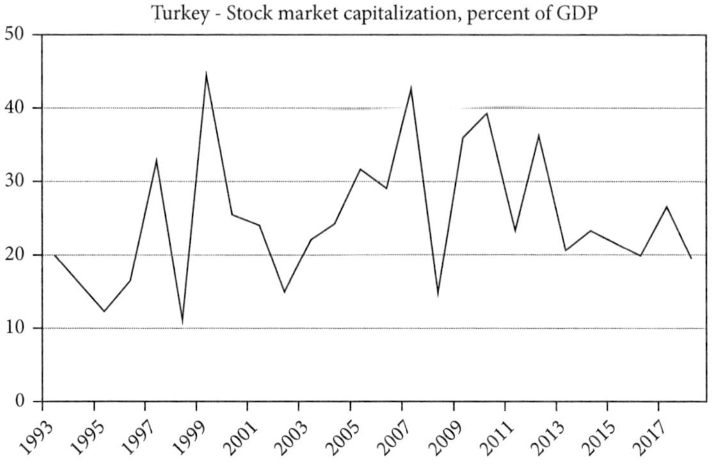

Fig. 1: The Stock Market Capitalization as a Share of GDP. Source: TGlobalEconomy.com, The World Bank

refers to the increasing role of financial movements, financial markets, financial actors, and financial institutions in the operation of local and international economies. Financialization has many dimensions and is related to many different economic enterprises (Epstein, 2005).

Another definition was made by Dore (2008). Financialization is a concept used for more or less different structural changes in industrialized world economies. Financialization, which is similar to globalization, has similar effects on changes in power, income, and wealth distribution on economic growth. Specifically, financialization is a process of economic restructuring in which institutional financial actors play an increasing role in national economies. In addition, financialization requires increased accumulation of profits through financial means, such as interest, dividends, and capital gains, rather than trading, commodity production, or nonfinancial services (Krippner, 2005, 2011).

The rise of the financial sector is also reflected in the increase in financial activity compared to actual economic activity measured by GDP. Figure 1 shows the stock market capitalization as a share of GDP for Turkey for the years 1993 until 2017. Stock market capitalization is in a permanent fluctuation. Sharp declines are particularly noteworthy during the crisis years.

Figure 2 presents the stock value traded as a share of GDP for Turkey for the years 1993 until 2018. It is very clear that stock value traded has increased during times of crisis.

Fig. 2: Stock Value Traded as a Share of GDP. Source: The World Bank

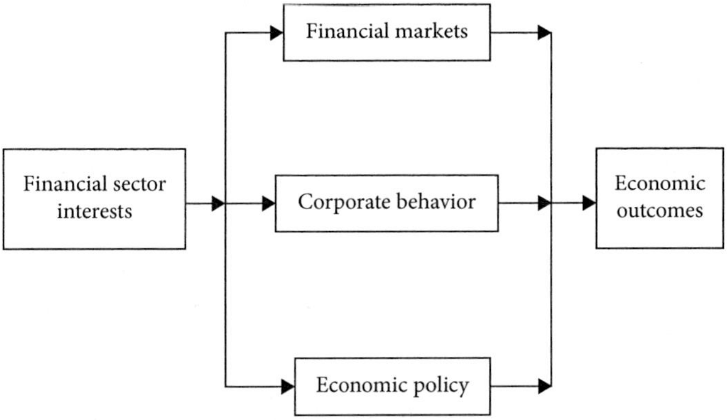

Fig. 3: Conduits of Financialization. Source: Palley (2007)

Financialization is important in terms of the scope of increased debt, changes in the functional distribution of income, wage stagnation, and increased income inequality. Changes in these factors will affect the structure of the economy, economic policy, and the behavior of companies (Palley, 2007: 15). Palley (2007) stated how the effect of financialization mechanics on the interests of financial sector works through three different channels. The first channel in Fig. 3 deals with the structure and functioning of financial markets. The second channel deals with the behavior of nonfinancial companies and the third channel deals

with economic policy. Thus, the economic results of the financialization process are shaped in line with the interests of the financial sector.

More specifically, financialization involves several intertwined processes (Kus, 2012): increasing share of financial sector in the economy, increased confidence of nonfinancial firms in financial activities as a source of income, a new corporate governance view that sees the firm as a bundle of tradable assets, and increased households' aim to generate income through financial markets as credit consumers or as buyers of investment products or to maintain living standards.

Krippner (2004) evaluated financialization in five different ways. First, financialization refers to an increase within the concept of shareholder value as a company management style. The second is the increasing dominance of capital market-based financial systems over bank-based financial systems. Third, the increasing economic and political power of the rent class. Fourth, financial transactions/trade is booming, thanks to increasing financial intermediaries and instruments.

Lapavistas (2013) defined financialization on the basis of four characteristics. These four characteristics are the integration of financial capital, banking system, financial elite, and workers into the financial system. On the basis of these four characteristics, financialization is based on a system shaped by more economic authority than intermediary institutions and practices and capital accumulation.

As stated above, there are many different dimensions and domains of financialization. It is critical for developing and developed countries to adapt to financialization which has national and international impacts. The next section provides and discusses the existing approaches to financialization.

2 An Overview of Financialization

Financialization was strengthened in the early 1980s by Ronald Reagan's efforts to remove barriers to economic growth brought on by labor, high taxes, and government regulations on capital in the United States and abroad (Brenner, 2006: 242). The financial sector is the first sector that comes to mind when financialization is mentioned with the liberalization of international capital flows and the stretching of the rules of the financial sector. This new financial outlook includes financial innovation ranging from money market funds to private equity and hedge funds. The financial sector of the economy includes financial instruments, financial institutions, and financial markets.

The effects of financialization on households, firms, banking sector, central bank, governments, and rest of world sectors continue to be the subject of

research. Financialization has a profound impact on the economies applying to external credit for financing the current account deficit. In particular, the impact of financialization on firms and households at the micro level is noticeable in developing countries. The firm's choice to finance investments and the current account deficit through external financing rather than savings so this behavior causes difficulties in the face of fluctuations in financial flows. The same effect is observed on households. The fact that households ignore savings and turn to consumption craze has brought some risks. The fact that individuals spend their expenses with financial instruments such as credit card has resulted in a debt cycle. The main components of these consumption habits of households are not only rational behavior but also socioeconomic and sociocultural changes. Another effect of financialization on households is related to income inequality. This relationship will be discussed in the next section.

Another area of influence of financialization is international. The financial sector has entered a process of transformation with the effects of neoliberalism and globalization. The liberalization of international capital flows has led to an increase in exchange rate fluctuations, resulting in a severe crisis in exchange rates. This has led to a debate on the effects of the liberalization of capital flows or, more generally, of financial globalization (Stockhammer, 2010). It is argued that financial globalization will benefit especially developing countries. The basis of this view is that capital flows from rich countries to poor countries will begin, and there will be a positive correlation between financial globalization and growth indicators. However, it is seen that financial globalization and liberalization often cause exchange rate crises and international imbalances caused by variable capital flows.

Financialization refers to two interconnected processes. The first process is to increase the importance of financial services firms in economic, social, and political terms (Davis, 2009). The second process is the trajectory associated with increased participation of nonfinancial firms in financial activities (Krippner, 2011, quoted Tomaskovic-Devey, Lin, & Meyers, 2015). Furthermore, according to Foster (2010), financialization can be defined as the shift of the center of gravity in the capitalist economy from production to finance in the long run. This change can be traced in each area of the five different indicators of the economy: increase in financial profits; increase in debt by GDP; growth of finance, insurance, and real estate sectors in national income; increase in financial instruments; and increasing role of financial bubbles.

The literature on financialization points to the negative and positive effects of financialization on both the real and financial sides of the economy. Greenwood and Scharfstein (2013) point to a large growth in the financial service sector in

the United States over the last 30 years, measured by the share of financial services in GDP, the amount of financial assets, employment, and average wages in the financial sector.

Dünhaupt (2016) provides a general discussion about the term "financialization" and provides some stylized facts that emphasize the rise of finance. Dünhaupt (2016) examines the fundamental arguments that lead to the crisis put forward within the Marxian framework and examines the financial tradition on the basis of two schools of thought in the Marxist tradition, which considers the final stage of capitalism. The wages have been stagnated, and income emphasizes the redistribution from labor to capital in the age of neoliberalism and financialization. However, the increase in income inequality suggests that it does not lead to a decline in consumption demand and an inadequate consumption crisis.

Correa and Vidal (2012) emphasize that the accumulation in the financialization process presents a structure that is difficult to manage, especially for environmental economies, and which does not allow long-term profitability of private companies and pregnant women.

Levy-Orlik (2012) argues that the financialization process causes transnational corporations to make strong financial decisions for redistribution rather than redistributing profits, regardless of the financing of their production activities.

Karwowski (2012) provides evidence that South African firms are overcapitalized that is, they keep their financial assets to a greater extent than they need in their productive activities and become the largest bank deposit holders.

Lapavitsas (2011) presents a financialization analysis based on classical Marxism. Financialization represents a systemic transformation of mature capitalist economies with three interrelated characteristics. First, large companies rely less on banks and acquire financial capacities. Secondly, banks shifted their activities towards mediation in open financial markets and dealing with households. Thirdly, households became increasingly involved in financial activities.

Aalbers (2008) approached finance in terms of housing and mortgage market and mortgage crisis. Financialization defines capital as the transformation of capital movements in primary, secondary, tertiary, or more markets.

Kotz (2008) analyzed the concepts of neoliberalism, globalization, and financialization in the context of the changing role of finance in the economy and found that the role of finance in economic activity has increased gradually.

Reich (2008) argues that the financialization process leads to increased risk and limitation of labor market mobility, especially on the primary labor market, which includes the labor force in the high-paid and social security system, with the effect of retirement and health assurance compared to the previous period.

3 Financialization and Income Inequality

Epstein (2005) were the first to express the relationship between financialization and income inequality. The 2008 global crisis has been the subject of research on how dangerous and large-scale consequences of financialization and income distribution injustice can be for each other as nurturing processes. Several factors contributed to the intensification of global inequality (Seguino, 2014): The most important feature of this process is the slowdown in wage increases and in some cases the decrease in real wages. A second factor contributing to increased inequality is the pressure of governments to reduce public sector spending on much-needed physical and social infrastructure, particularly roads, immunization, rural health clinics, agricultural extension, and education. Another source of increasing inequality and the resulting shortage of demand is the exchange between central banks within the policy framework.

Tridico (2017) described the relationship between financialization and income inequality under two headings.

- *Inequality can weaken aggregate demand and drive the economy because high-income groups spend a smaller share of income; moreover, income inequality increases financial instability because it increases the demand for credit, and this can destabilize aggregate demand, especially when determining loan rates.*
- *Inequality is increased by enabling financial development, credit consumption, and the financialization of the economy, i.e., the expansion of debts and the tightening of wage share through reduction. The distribution of labour and profit among shareholders, the reduction of flexible labour markets, and the welfare state increase income fragility and reduces the purchasing power of workers.*

Neoliberal policies increase income injustice with the transformation of economic policies. The correlation between these mutually strengthened trends is a challenge in modeling determinants of increased income inequality. Figure 4 illustrates the relationship between financialization and income inequality.

There are positive and negative effects of financialization on income inequality. Kuş (2012) describes the effects of financialization on income inequality by Palley (2007), Kremp (2012), and Tomaskovic-Devey and Lin (2011):

- *Financing expansion and the productivity of the real economy have involved in the last few decades. The shrinking profitability of the nonfinancial sector is likely to result in shrinking net wages for many middle-class and blue-collar workers operating in productive industries.*
- *The shift from the real economy as the dominant source of profit to the financial sector has contributed to the weakening of certain policies and institutions,*

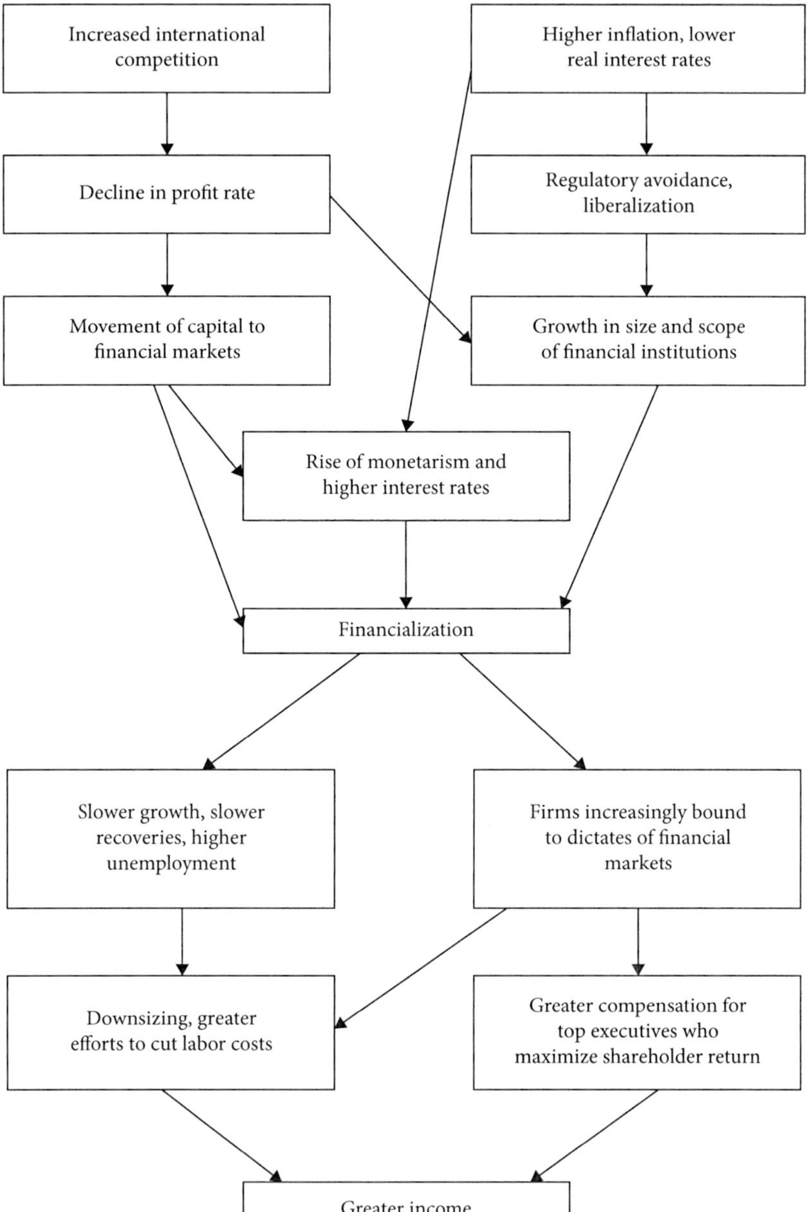

Fig. 4: Causal Chart Linking Financialization and Income Inequality. Source: Van Arnum and Naples (2013: 1166)

possibly helping trade unions and minimum wage laws to control income imbalance.

- *The dependence of nonfinancial firms on the financial sector and the market requires a new corporate governance structure that emphasizes the harmony of the interests of shareholders and managers that always focus on short-term profits.*
- *The stock market boom from the late 1990s to the early 2000s probably contributed to the highest revenue concentration (Kremp, 2012, quoted by Kus, 2012).*
- *Government policies aimed at encouraging the growth and profitability of the financial sector are also likely to have effects on inequality.*

There is an inseparable link between financialization and global inequality. This link is reinforced by the changes in financial capital structure, technological innovations, ideological orientations and values, and the dynamics of global capitalism. The shift from the structure of the global economy to production and financialization also has implications for low-skilled workers as well as small-scale industrial owners who do not have access to credit and loans (Oloruntoba, 2015). There are many reasons underlying the increase in stagnation and income inequality in the literature (Gordon & Dew-Becker, 2007; Levy & Temin, 2007; quoted by Palley 2007; Palley, 2000). Erosion of trade unions, minimum wage, and labor market solidarity; globalization and trade; migration; and skill-biased technical change factors are among these factors. Financialization argues that many of these factors should be linked and interpreted as part of a new economic structure that is clearly encouraged by the interests of the financial sector (Palley, 2007).

The stagnation of wages and changes in personal income distribution were accompanied by changes in the functional distribution of income, and these recent changes revealed the role of financialization. Figure 5 shows the national income tree that explains how national income can be divided into payments as wages and capital income. While wages can be allocated to payments to managers and workers, capital revenues can be allocated to profit and interest payments, and profits can be allocated to financial and nonfinancial sector profits.

Numerous studies have been studying on financialization and income inequality. Stockhammer (2009) was the first to discover the contribution of global financialization to the declining wage share of income in 22 high-income countries between 1979 and 2007. Zalewski and Whalen (2010) argued that financialization has contributed to increased income inequality in 15 European countries, Canada, Japan, and USA since the 1990s. Charpe and Tobin (2011)

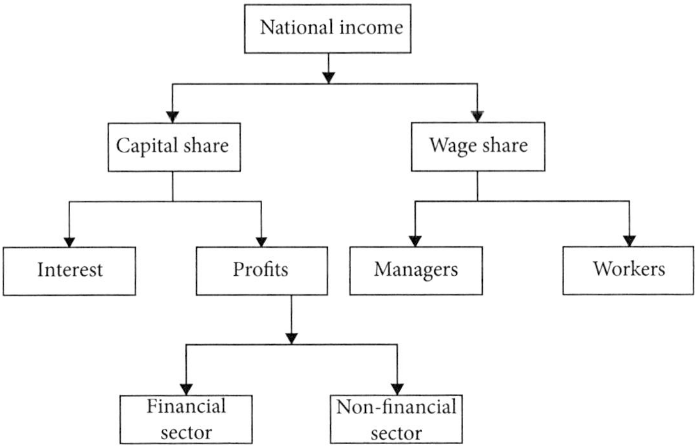

Fig. 5: Financialization and the Functional Distribution of Income. Source: Palley (2007: 12)

examined the impact of the financialization measure on labor share in 16 high-income countries between 1981 and 2005. Bentolila and Saint-Paul (2003) stated that technological change, globalization, and transformation in labor market institutions are the key determinants of wage share and revealed the first two most appropriate factors. Hein (2012) examines certain channels of effect between 2012 financialization and reduced wage share. According to this study, the main link between financialization and functional distribution emerges with the bargaining power of employees. Onaran, Engelbert, and Lucas (2011) stated that financialization and functional distribution of income had a significant impact on total demand in the USA, although it did not have a significant effect on total demand and income distribution.

Tomaskovic-Devey and Lin (2011) have presented an econometric model since the 1970s, indicating that between 5.8 and 6.6 trillion dollars of other sectors in the economy, including labor and taxpayers, have been transferred to the financial sector. Lin and Tomaskovic-Devey (2013) find that in the time-series cross-sectional data in the sector, the dependence on increasing financial income, in the long run, is related to the reduction of labor. Chusseau and Dumont (2012) show that globalization and changes in labor market institutions that weaken the welfare state explain the inequality in a group of 12 rich countries.

Conclusion

The aim of this study is to review and introduce the literature from various perspectives focusing on financialization and income inequality. Numerous studies have shown that financialization leads to income inequality. It is clear that wages become stagnant due to financialization and the income distribution is redistributed from labor to capital. The way to reduce inequality requires not only the improvement of the leverage ratio of labor interests but also the growth of the financial sector (Van Arnum & Naples, 2013).

Financialization and income inequality is one of the most important transformations of developed economies in recent years. It is thought that a new era has begun with financialization and that there will be no crises with financialization. However, with the recent global crisis, financial markets, which have reached enormous dimensions, constitute one of the biggest threats to the global economy. In particular, financial crises increased income inequality. Despite the crises, financialization is increasing its importance. Although policymakers impose restrictions and prohibitions against financing, especially firms and households are increasingly strengthening their ties with the financial sector and diversifying their financial transactions.

Bibliography

Aalbers, M. B. (2008). *The financialization of home and the mortgage market crisis*. New York: The Editors and W.S. Maney & Son Ltd.

Assa, J. (2012). Financialization and its consequences: The OECD experience. *Finance Research, 1*(1), 35–39.

Bentolila, S., & Saint-Paul, G. (2003). Explaining movements in the labor share. *B.E. Journal of Macroeconomics, 3*, 1–33.

Brenner, R. (2006). *The economics of global turbulence: The advanced capitalist economies from long boom to long downturn, 1945–2005*. Cambridge, MA: Harvard University Press/Verso.

Charpe, M., with S. Tobin. (2011). The labour share of income: Determinants and potential contribution to exiting the financial crisis. In R. Torres (Ed.), *World of work report 2011* (pp. 55–73), International Labour Office, Switzerland.

Chusseau, N., & Dumont, M. (2012). *Growing income inequalities in advanced countries* (ECINEQ Working Paper 2012–260).

Correa, E., & Vidal, G. (2012). Financialization and global financial crisis in Latin American countries. *Journal of Economic Issues, 46*(2), 541–548.

Davis, G. F. (2009). *Managed by the markets: How finance re-shaped America*. Oxford: Oxford University Press.

Dore, R. (2008). Financialization of the global economy. *Industrial and Corporate Change, 17*(6), 1097–1112.

Dünhaupt, P. (2016). *Financialization and the crises of capitalism* (Working Paper No. 67/2016). Berlin: Institute for International Political Economy.

Epstein, G. A. (Ed.). (2005). *Financialization and the world economy*. Cheltenham, UK: Edward Elgar.

Foster, J. B. (2010). The financialization of accumulation. *Monthly Review, 62*(5), 1.

Gordon, R. J., & Dew-Becker, I. (2007). Unresolved issues in the rise of American inequality. *Brookings Panel on Economic Activity*, Washington, DC, *September, 7*, 207.

Greenwood, R., & Scharfstein, D. (2013). The growth of finance. *Journal of Economic Perspectives,* 27(2), 3–28.

Hein, E. (2012). *The macroeconomics of finance-dominated capitalism—And its crisis*. London: Edward Elgar.

Hyde, A., Vachon, T., & Wallace, M. (2018). Financialization, income inequality, and redistribution in 18 affluent democracies, 1981–2011. *Social Currents, 5*(2), 193–211.

Karwowski, E. (2012). Financial operations of South African listed firms: Growth and financial stability in an emerging market setting. Paper presented at *III Conferencia international do IESE*, Mozambique, September 3–4.

Kotz, D. M., (2008). *Neoliberalism and financialization*. Amherst: University of Massachusetts Press.

Kremp, P. (2012). Bubble and inequality: Financialization, diffusion and portfolio returns of US households, 1989–2005. Working paper, presented at the Dublin Workshops on Financialisation, Consumption, and Social Welfare Politics, May 24–26, Dublin.

Krippner, G. (2004). *What is financialization?* Los Angeles: University of California.

Krippner, G. R. (2005). The financialization of the American economy. *Socio-economic Review, 3*(2), 173–208.

Krippner, G. R. (2011). *Capitalizing on crisis: The political origins of the rise of finance*. Cambridge, MA: Harvard University Press.

Kus, B. (2012). Financialisation and income inequality in OECD nations: 1995–2007. *The Economic and Social Review, 43*(4, Winter), 477–495.

Lapavitsas, C. (2011). Theorizing financialization. *Work, employment and society*, *25*(4), 611–626.

Lapavitsas, C. (2013). *Profiting without producing: How finance exploits us all*. London: Verso Books.

Levy, F., & Temin, P. (2007). *Inequality and institutions in 20th century America*. Cambridge, MA: National Bureau of Economic Research.

Levy-Orlik, N. (2012). Effects of financialization on the structure of production and nonfinancial private enterprises: The case of Mexico. *Journal of Post Keynesian Economics*, *35*(2), 235–254.

Lin, K., & Tomaskovic-Devey, D. (2013). Financialization and US income inequality: 1970–2008. *American Journal of Sociology*, *118*(5), 1284–1329.

Oloruntoba, S. (2015). Politics of Financialisation and Inequality: Transforming Global Relations for Inclusive Development. Africa Development, 40(3), 121–137.

Onaran, Ö., Engelbert, S., & Lucas, G. (2011). Financialisation, income distribution and aggregate demand in the USA. *Cambridge Journal of Economics*, *35*(4), 637–661.

Palley, T. I. (2000). *Plenty of nothing: The downsizing of the American dream and the case for structural Keynesianism*. Princeton: Princeton University Press.

Palley, T. I. (2007). Financialization: what it is and why it matters (Working Paper No. 525). Finance-led Capitalism? Macroeconomic Effects of Changes in the Financial Sector, Berlin, 2007. London: Metropolis.

Palley, T. I. (2013). Financialization: What it is and why it matters. In *Financialization* (pp. 17–40). London: Palgrave Macmillan. *Perspectives*, *27*(2), 3–28.

Reich, M. (2008). Labor market segmentation: 1970 to 2000. In *Segmented labor markets and labor mobility*. London: Edward Elgar.

Seguino, S. (2014). Financialization, distribution, and inequality. In G. Sen & M. Durano (Eds.), *The remaking of social contracts: Global feminists in the 21st century*. London: Zed Books.

Stiglitz, J. E. (2012). *The price of inequality: How today's divided society endangers our future*. New York: W.W. Norton.

Stockhammer, E. (2009). *Determinants of functional income distribution in OECD countries*. Dusseldorf: Macroeconomic Policy Institute study commissioned by the Hans Böckler Foundation.

Stockhammer, E. (2010). Financialization and the global economy. *Political Economy Research Institute Working Paper*, *242*, 40.

Tomaskovic-Devey, D., & Lin, K. (2011). Income dynamics, economic rents, and the Financialization of the US economy. *American Sociological Review, 76*(4), 538–559.

Tomaskovic-Devey, D., Lin, K. H., & Meyers, N. (2015). Did financialization reduce economic growth?. *Socio-Economic Review, 13*(3), 525–548.

Tridico, P. (2017). The determinants of income inequality in OECD countries. *Cambridge Journal of Economics, 42*(4), 1009–1042. University Press.

Van Arnum, B. M., & Naples, M. I. (2013). Financialization and income Inequality in the United States, 1967–2010. *American Journal of Economics and Sociology, 72*(5), 1158–1182.

Zalewski, D. A., & Whalen, C. J. (2010). Financialization and income inequality: A post Keynesian institutionalist analysis. *Journal of Economic Issues, 44*(3), 757–777.

Derya Yalçın

Chapter Six: Pricing System in National and Global Markets

Abstract: Businesses can control the internal environmental conditions, but this is not the case for external environmental conditions. The crisis in international capital markets in recent days is the closest example. For this reason, the speed of response of the enterprises to the current conditions becomes important. The issue of price is also in the reaction area of the enterprises. Therefore, it is not possible to succeed by adhering to a single price strategy and/or policy.Therefore, in this part of our book, we will first examine the pricing strategies of capital assets and the influencing factors of pricing in both national and international markets, and consider pricing strategies which are new product pricing strategies, product mix strategies, and price adjustment strategies (discount and allowance pricing, segmented pricing, psychological pricing, promotional pricing, geographical pricing, dynamic pricing, and international pricing); and we will examine four price methods: cost-based pricing, demand-based pricing, competition-based pricing, and customer value–based pricing method.Also we will see the strategies used in international pricing: dumping and transfer pricing.

Keywords: Price, pricing strategies, pricing methods, capital assets, price adjustment

Introduction

Companies that provide the goods and services component that can meet the needs of people constitute the cornerstone of the national economies (Yağcı et al., 2014).

In a modern economy, companies and stock markets constitute an important part of the financial system (Santomero, 2002: 104).

An effective pricing process will reward well-managed and profitable firms and make their shares more valuable. This mechanism will lead to new investments with lower capital costs and will accelerate economic growth in total (Leigh, 1997). Information that gives firms stock prices encourages firms to make investment decisions in more productive areas, and so it accelerates the economic growth (Dow & Gorton, 1995).

Pricing is a sensitive decision area. The price is about the money that will come out of the consumer's pocket so it is the first remarkable feature when buying a good or service (Karafakıoğlu, 2015: 53). There is also a close relationship between price and firm value.

1 Relationship between Financial System and Pricing in Business

Price in economic theory is defined as a variable that directs resources, attracts businessmen from one area to another, and guides consumers in maximizing benefits (İslamoğlu, 2013: 403).

In the narrowest sense, price is the amount of money received for a product or service. In a broad sense, price is the sum of the values that customers leave to gain the benefits of using a product or service. However, price remains one of the most important factors that determine the market share and profitability of a firm (Kotler and Armstrong, 2018: 308).

In free economies, price is a means of regulating economic life. It acts as a balance element in the system (Stanton, 1994: 411).

Therefore, it is decided whether an economy is bad or not by looking at prices. Theoretically, businesses cannot intervene in prices under perfect competition. They have to accept the market price. In the monopolistic market structure, the enterprise applies the price that will provide the highest profit to itself based on the price-demand relationship. Price decisions in oligopoly market structures are a game (İslamoğlu, 2013: 403).

Economic conditions affect firms' financial structures and may have a strong impact on pricing strategies. Economic factors such as boom or recession, inflation, and interest rates affect pricing decisions because they affect consumer spending, consumer perceptions of the price and value of the product, and the company's costs of producing and selling products (Kotler & Armstrong, 2018: 323).

Therefore, cash inflow, profitability ratio, and capital structure within the financial structure of the firms will be affected.

The price of a good also affects the price of production factors. Wages, rent, interest, and profits are affected by the price. This relationship is important in terms of regulating the resource allocation in financial structure and economies (Yükselen, 2017: 207).

Price is very important for businesses. This is because the price directly affects the position of the company in the market and its market share (Stanton, 1994: 411).

Pricing objectives or targets are generally business and marketing objectives, because management strives to achieve certain marketing objectives, not only at price but also through all other decision variables. The main business and marketing objectives that an enterprise wants to achieve when determining prices

for a particular product are in the light of some research on this subject (Mucuk, 2010: 155).

- *Current profit maximization*
- *Target profit*
- *Market share*
- *Revenue maximization*
- *And taking the gilt off the market*

Also Oluç (1988: 9–10) added that

- *Maintaining company life*
- *Achieving financial success*
- *Meet fast cash flow requirements*
- *Provide targeted return on investment*
- *Profit maximization.*

Generally, the main purpose of the firms was to ensure maximum profit until the beginning of the 20th century. As a result of the developments and criticisms directed to this, the aim of the firms is defined as maximizing the financial structure of the firm and maximizing the value of the firm for the partners. In order for a company to survive and gain competitive advantage and maintain this advantage, it is necessary to have a strong competitive ability (Aydeniz, 2009: 264).

Business finance also adapts the financial resources of the enterprise in terms of type and amount to cover all decisions which are necessary for the effective use of capital resources. Under these decisions, financial management has to prioritize four objectives. These objectives are as follows (Usta, 2014: 21):

- *Creating the appropriate financial structure*
- *Protecting the security of equity*
- *Ensure an adequate profit and profitability*
- *Maintaining the liquidity of the company.*

Price has an important place in the competition between the enterprises (İslamoğlu, 2013: 403). The firm also needs financial performance measures in order to determine this situation. Through financial performance analysis, firms can effectively carry out healthy decision-making, planning, and audit functions. When the financial performance analysis is performed successfully, the performance of the enterprise is also accurately reflected. Companies can perform successful financial performance management with financial performance criteria and increase the value of the firm. Financial performance is important for

the company managers, and people who will invest in the company (Aydeniz, 2009: 265).

In all analyses used in the analysis of financial performance and financial structure, price which is the basic building block of sales plays an important role.

Because among the purposes of pricing as well as those listed above, there are also objectives such as achieving the targeted repayment rate through sales or investment and resisting competition (Cemalcılar, 1987: 256).

The enterprise may aim to achieve a certain amount of cash flow through either its estimated sales or investment in the production and marketing of the goods in question.

However, it should not neglect to consider the return period. This decision will be based on investment volume, expected sales in the market, and the course of economic conditions. In markets where economic conditions are stable, long-term objectives are easier to achieve, so the enterprise may consider, for example, a five-year period in such a market. In other words, the business may want to pay for itself within five years. In the light of the forecasted sales, the entity may choose to set a price that will allow a certain percentage of revenue to flow to the entity (Yükselen, 2016: 246).

Price policy objectives – business, commercial, and customers – can be grouped into three groups (Bruhn, 2000: 166):

- *In terms of business: Increase in version and market shares, improvement in profit and profitability, increase in profit contribution and return on investment (ROI).*
- *From the commercial point of view: Growth in existing commercial channels, meeting market expectations, increasing distribution level and providing more space on the shelf, and securing the same price practices in different distribution channels.*
- *From the customer's point of view: Price comparison with competing products, determining price suitability, improving price fairness by comparing price and product quality, and influencing price perception.*

Liquidity, inventory turnover rate, account receivables turnover rate, current asset turnover rate, and equity capital turnover rate are used in the analysis of the financial structure of an enterprise due to the effects of price level and price changes on stocks and sales as well as issues such as product quality and brand awareness. Profitability as well as the price indirectly affect the calculation of ratios.

The ability of enterprises to maintain their assets, have a certain market share, grow, and achieve their goals is closely related to their financial structures. Companies that want to have a good financial structure should have good cash

flow, and inventory turnover should be optimal. Pricing that has an impact on these issues should be meticulously determined.

At the same time, pricing is not only an important issue on the sale of goods and services, but also it is important on the sale of capital assets.

Shortly, the price is an important decision variable in financial decision indicators; financial analysis (profitability ratios, activity ratios, share performance events); and dividend distribution in both national and international markets.

Therefore, in this part of our book, we will first examine the pricing strategies of capital assets and the influencing factors of pricing in goods and services both nationally and internationally, and consider pricing strategies and methods of goods and services individually.

2 Capital Assets and Pricing

In general, exchange rate, money supply, industrial production index, inflation, gold price, and foreign trade balance are used in the researches which are about the relationship between capital assets and macroeconomic variables (Özer et al., 2011: 165).

Franck and Young's (1972) research is one of the first to examine the relationship between stock prices and exchange rates and showed that there was no significant interaction between the variables as a result of the study. Although many studies have been conducted on this subject, no consensus has been reached. Aggarwal (1981), Solnik (1987), Roll (1992), and Phylaktis and Ravazzollo (2005) found the existence of a positive relationship between stock prices and exchange rate variables. Soenen and Hennigar (1988) and Kim (2003) have found a negative relationship between these variables. Chow et al. (1997), Bahmani et al. (1992), Nieh and Lee (2001), and Ozair (2006) stated that no relationship exists (Özer et al., 2011: 165).

When we look at the scientific researches which are done in Turkey, Kasman (2003) found that there is a stable relationship between stock prices and exchange rate in the long run. Özmen's (2007) research results show that there is a bidirectional causality between variables, except for the periods 1989–1994 and 1994–1999. The causality test results for the period 1989–1994 and 1994–1999 show a one-way causality from the exchange rate to the stocks. Kıran (2009) shows that there is a cointegration relationship between exchange rate and stock prices in the long run. Toda Yamamoto causality analysis results reveal the existence of a bidirectional causality relationship between variables for the period 1990–2008 and 1995–2008 (Özer et al., 2011: 166).

According to Altıntaş and Tombuk's (2011) results, there is a long-term relationship between stock prices and growth, real exchange rate, large money supply, and international reserves. In addition, the relationship between equities and real exchange rate was found to be positive (Doğru & Recepoğlu, 2013: 20).

In public offerings, intermediary institutions may sometimes commit to the issuers to sell their shares as soon as they are placed on the market. In order to fulfill these commitments, they try to facilitate the sale by determining the prices of stocks below their real value. This situation seems to be one of the factors leading to low pricing (Hirt, 2004: 227).

According to Beatty and Ritter and Rock (1986), low pricing is often associated with future uncertainty.

We examine the reasons for low pricing in capital assets as follows:

- *Transition to market economy with modern financial markets (Hirt, 2004; Dongwei & Belton, 1999)*
- *High economic uncertainties (Rock, 1994; Beatty & Ritter, 1996; Dongwei & Belton, 1999)*
- *Bribery and corruption (Dongwei & Belton, 1999)*
- *Extension of the period between the announcement of the public offering and the first trading day (Dongwei & Belton, 1999)*
- *Investor demand (Kirkulak & Davis, 2005)*
- *Public sectors (Huibers and Raat, 1994) are the main factors for low pricing in capital assets.*

3 Factors Affecting Pricing

In a business one of the most important and complex decisions that managers must take are decisions related to the pricing of products and services. If consumers perceive the prices offered by the business as high, they may turn to the products of competing companies.

If the price is low, the profitability of the enterprise may decrease. Therefore, the highest level of attention and care should be taken when making pricing decisions in enterprises (Peter & Donnelly, 1998: 195).

In determining their price strategies, businesses must consider not only their final consumers but also their distributors and dealers, which are intermediary customers. Another factor is the competitors. They must also consider how their competitors will react to the price they will set. In addition, businesses should consider the owners of various factors that provide raw materials, labor, and

credit. As an important party that affects price decisions, it shows its effect in various forms and situations in government (Mucuk, 2010: 158).

Services are not produced in the factory so they are intagible. Also service firms are faced with complex pricing decisions because services have infinite varieties. (Öztürk, 2017: 73).

Cost is the another most important affect factor on the price and and also cost act the success of the company in the market. Costs can be divided into two groups: indirect (insurance, building and land taxes, communication, maintenance-repair, labor, depreciation, and electricity expenses) and direct (expenses directly incurred for the acquisition of goods or services). Cost expenses can be grouped into two groups as variable and fixed expenses (Yükselen, 2016: 209). Other factors that affect pricing are:

- *Legal regulations (determination of upper and lower price, customs clearance, etc.)*
- *Supply and demand*
- *The structure of the market*
- *Consumer buying behaviors*
- *Economical situation*
- *The quality of the goods*
- *Pricing purposes.*

In international marketing, İslamoğlu indicated price affecting factors this way (2014: 325);

- *Market entry strategies*
- *Country of manufacture*
- *The aim of the company in the international arena*
- *Distribution strategies and costs*
- *Geographical, cultural, and economic differences*
- *Product life cycle*
- *Quality and image of the product*
- *Barriers to entry*
- *Feature of the market*
- *Exchange rate fluctuations.*

In addition to these:

- *The possibility of deterioration or loss of value of products*
- *Seasonal sales*
- *Marketing and sales costs*

- *Turnover rate of sales or inventories affects the pricing.*

4 Pricing Methods

Cost, demand, and competition are the most commonly used pricing methods in the pricing process. In determining the base price, the cost determines the price floor and the consumer or the buyer's demand status determines the price ceiling. Because the enterprise cannot make profit in the first one and cannot make sales in the second. Business managers in the market determine the price by choosing one of the following three methods (Nakip et al., 2012: 162):

- *Cost-based pricing*
- *Demand-based pricing*
- *Competition-based pricing*
- *Customer value–based pricing method.*

4.1 Cost-Based Pricing Method

In pricing based on cost, the business does not take into account global competition or the structure of the market.

Companies often use cost-based pricing when selling to countries outside the parent country. Cost-based pricing method is based on internal (material, labor, etc.) and external cost analysis (insurance, transportation, etc.) (Keegan & Green, 2013: 327). These costs may vary from country to country. Because transportation, promotion, and distribution costs of each country differentiate the cost of the product (Benli, 2006). In international markets, extra costs and expenses such as transportation, fees, and insurance arise. If the manufacturer is responsible for them, these items must be taken into account.

In order to apply cost-based pricing, detailed cost information is required. Costs will not be realistic unless accurate and timely detailed cost information is reached.

There are two types of calculation methods. First, the cost plus and the second is target pricing.

4.1.1 Cost-Plus Pricing Method

The simplest pricing method is cost-plus pricing – adding a standard mark-up to the cost of the product. Construction companies, for example, submit job bids by estimating the total project cost and adding a standard mark-up for profit (Kotler et al., 1999: 701).

In practice, it is seen that the pricing approach is generally used based on cost. Both manufacturers, wholesalers and retailers sell the product by adding a certain profit to the unit cost. The formula is as follows (Karafakıoğlu, 1974: 41):

Sales Price = Cost + (Cost x Profit Percentage)

4.2 Target Pricing Method

In the pricing method based on the target profit, companies try to determine the prices in order to realize the targeted profit. In short, it can be defined as determining the selling price of the products in a way that provides a certain level of income to the producers. The aim of target pricing is to create the production process that will provide the desired profit.

Targeted Cost = Targeted Prıce - Expected Profıt

The target sales price and sales volume comes from information obtained from customers. The target profit is determined by looking at the desired profit rates throughout the life of the product. The target cost is the difference between the two. Market and cost characteristics play an important role in using target pricing. Under increasing competition, firms cannot control prices. In a competitive environment, it is the market that sets prices; and for businesses that ignore it, it is expensive. Therefore, when calculating the target cost, the estimated market price is taken into account. The role of product costs emerges during the planning and design phase. Once a product is designed and sent to production, it may not be possible to carry out studies that will significantly change the cost. Because after this stage, the type of cost changes (Bayar, 2012: 17).

4.3 Demand-Based Pricing

Demand pricing is often used in national and international markets by companies that develop and market goods that represent new cutting-edge technologies. Because these goods face a wide demand, their substitutes are not numerous. In this case, the firm has a monopoly power to determine its prices freely (Karafakıoğlu, 2008: 179).

Demand flexibility is one of the most important points in pricing. ***Demand elasticity*** of price is to determine how much demand will change despite price change. When the sales price of a product decreases, the amount of demand increases.

In case of ***inelastic demand***, the demand for a product is not sensitive to price changes and the increase in price leads to an increase in total revenue. It occurs when there is not much competition. In case of elastic demand, the

demand for the product is sensitive to price changes and causes a decrease in total revenue.

In demand-based pricing, the product is priced considering the demand for the product. If the demand for the product is high, a high price is put on the product; but if the demand for the product is low, the price of the product is low (Korkmaz et al., 2009: 406).

4.4 Competition-Based Pricing Method

Cost and demand pricing does not adequately take into account the competition in the market. For this reason, companies are going to make price decisions by considering the prices applied by competitors.

The basis of this method is that the entity determines its prices by looking at the competitors' prices. The price may be kept slightly higher or lower, provided that it remains within a certain percentage of the competition price. The most prominent feature of the competition-based method is that the firm does not try to maintain a relationship between price and cost or demand. The method has two main applications (Mucuk, 2010: 164):

- *Based on current price (market price)*
- *Closed envelope procedure.*

4.4.1 Based on Current Price (Market Price)

This method is very common in oligopoly markets. Businesses do not pay much attention to changes in demand or costs to their goods; they change the price by following the market leader and try to keep it at the average price level seen in the industry (Mucuk, 2010: 165).

4.4.2 Closed Envelope Procedure

It is used in contracting works taken under big contracts, especially in government tenders. This is required by law in public procurement procedures in Turkey, but this method is also used in large private enterprises. In this method, enterprises that offer products or services bid to the tenderer in a sealed envelope (Mucuk, 2010: 165).

4.5 Customer Value-Based Pricing Method

In value-based pricing, the starting point is how customers perceive "value." The customer accepts to pay according to value of the product. Therefore, they will

naturally choose the lowest price among the products of companies offering similar values. At this point, marketing management offer distinctive features that over the customer expectations if it is suitable for the customer's perception of value, they accept the price and make the payment. These distinctive features are offered for sale in the enriched product, and for service, is offered for sale in supportive services (Yükselen, 2017: 228).

5 Pricing Strategies

The price the company charges will fall somewhere between one that is too low to produce a profit and one that is too high to produce any demand. Customer perception of product's value determines the ceiling price. If the customer understands that the product has a value below the price they have paid, they will not buy the product. Likewise, product costs set the floor for a product's price. If the company prices the product below its costs, the company's profits will suffer (Kotler & Armstrong, 2018: 309).

5.1 New Product Pricing Strategies

Pricing strategies usually change as the product passes through its life cycle. The introductory stage is especially challenging. Companies bringing out a new product face the challenge of setting prices for the first time. They can choose between two broad strategies: market-skimming pricing and market-penetration pricing (Kotler et al., 2017: 332).

5.1.1 Market-Skimming Pricing

Price is an integral part of positioning strategy. The market-skimming strategy is part of an attempt to reach a market segment that is willing to pay a high price for a particular product or a customized product. Companies that follow a differentiation strategy or position their products for high-income groups often use a market-skimming strategy.

The market-skimming strategy is appropriate when production capacity and competition are limited at the entry stage of the product life cycle. By deliberately setting the price, the demand is limited to innovators and early adopters who are willing to pay the price. As the product life cycle grows, competition increases and producers start to break prices (Keagan & Green, 2015: 320–321).

5.1.2 Market-Penetration Pricing

Business may aim to increase its market share instead of increasing sales revenue and profit rapidly in entry and growth periods. By aiming for a healthy

development in the long term, it keeps its price low and enables more consumers to buy. In order to implement the market entry strategy (Yükselen, 2017: 221):

- *Demand must be elastic against price*
- *Competitors are likely to enter the market in a short time*
- *The market segment that can pay a high price for this good or service should not be satisfactory.*

5.2 Product Mix Strategies

Product mix strategies are five strategies (Kotler et al., 2017: 315):

- ***Product line pricing:*** *setting prices across an entire product line*
- ***Optional-product pricing:*** *pricing optional or accessory products sold with the main product*
- ***Captive-product pricing:*** *pricing products that must be used with the main product*
- ***By-product pricing:*** *pricing low-value by-products to get rid of or make money on them*
- ***Product bundle pricing:*** *pricing bundles of products sold together.*

6 Price Adjustment Strategies

Companies usually adjust their basic prices to account for various customer differences and changing situations. Here we examine the seven price adjustment strategies summarized in discount and allowance pricing, segmented pricing, psychological pricing, promotional pricing, geographical pricing, dynamic pricing, and international pricing (Kotler et al., 2017: 336).

6.1 Discount and Allowance Pricing

A discounted price policy is the reduction of the specified basic price by a certain amount or rate, depending on certain conditions. This policy is used in four different ways, especially to encourage intermediary businesses in their sales efforts (İslamoğlu, 2013: 426–428):

- ***Functional discount:*** *the purpose of the functional reduction is to attract intermediary businesses to goods and sales efforts, leaving an incentive to profit. The manufacturer first determines the last price to be sold to the consumer. It then goes backwards and sets the price that leaves a certain profit margin to intermediaries of all levels.*

- ***Amount reduction:*** *instead of reducing the list price to increase production and make production more smooth, they give customers the amount of goods at a certain rate of the amount they buy.*
- ***Seasonal discount*** *is a policy to encourage the sale of goods and services whose sales depend largely on the seasons. It is a common policy in hotels and apparel industry.*
- ***The early payment discount*** *is discounted at a certain rate for each early payment to be made by setting the price at a certain term.*

6.2 Segmented Pricing

Companies will often adjust their basic prices to allow for differences in customers, products, and locations. In segmented pricing, the company sells a product or service at two or more prices, even though the difference in prices is not based on differences in costs (Kotler et al., 2005: 697).

- Customer-segment pricing: Customers pay different prices for the same product and service according to their age, location, and training. Museums, for example, will charge a lower admission for students, senior citizens, and young people.
- Product-form pricing: Different models of the product are priced differently; but it is not about the their costs, it is about product's features.
- Location pricing: It is used especially in theaters and concerts, different places are priced differently.
- Time pricing: Prices vary by day, hour, and month. For example, last-minute flights.

6.3 Psychological Pricing

It is a widely used policy especially in retailing. The tactics that provide psychological superiority to the business are as follows (Mucuk, 2010: 167):

- ***Fractional pricing:*** *after the price of the product is calculated, rough calculation is not done, and gives the price at a fraction of the price just below this figure.*
- ***Fixed pricing:*** *it is the same price for many years, with the profit percentage decreasing over time.*
- ***Prestige pricing:*** *keeping the price high is the psychological placement of the image of quality to consumers through price.*
- ***Pricing via quantity discount:*** *it is a kind of hidden price tactic which is realized by reducing the amount of products and shortening the time in the service sector but not changing the price.*

6.4 Promotional Pricing

It is a common price policy used by both manufacturers and retailers. The purpose of this price policy is to provide price reductions for many products and attract customer's attention and increase brand awareness. The sale of the product is realized below the usual profit margin or at the cost price in a short time.

- ***Price leaders:*** *short-term sale of the products of famous brands.*
- ***Special event pricing:*** *price discounts on special occasions such as mothers day, fathers day, Christmas, etc.*
- ***Special interest payment plan:*** *it is a pricing policy used especially in automobile and home sales.*
- ***Artificial discount:*** *give the product a non-real price and then show it as a discount on this price.*

6.5 Geographical Pricing

The business that sells the product also considers the product reaching the buyer in pricing. If the shipping cost increases, the share of this in total variable costs also increases. This leads to different price applications such as "FOB price," "single delivery price," and "regional delivery prices." FOB price is a commonly used price practice in foreign trade. At the single delivery price, the business undertakes the transportation costs and the same price is applied everywhere, regardless of region. In the region delivery price, the price varies from region to region (Cemalcılar, 2000: 181–182).

6.6 Dynamic Pricing

It is used in product pricing especially in sectors with high initial cost, consumable capacity, short sales period, and price-sensitive demand structure. Exhaustible capacity is generally seen in the service sector. Price varies depending on demand level, customer type, and time. This strategy is used for football, concert tickets, hotels, transportation (bus, sea, air), and hotels' peak period; and off-season pricing is applied in different online auctions (Ustaahmetoğlu, 2014: 240).

6.7 International Pricing

The company may have different marketing objectives in various global markets, which require changes in pricing strategy. The price that a company should charge in a specific country depends on factors such as economic factors, competitive situations, laws and regulations, and the nature of the wholesaling and retailing system (Kotler et al., 2017: 324).

Companies can use three different approaches to take in pricing efforts in global markets (Keegan & Green, 2015: 337):

- ***Extension or ethnocentric pricing:*** *in this pricing strategy, the unit price of the product must be the same regardless of the country where the buyer is located. In this case, the importer has to pay the freight and fees.*
- ***Polycentric pricing:*** *subsidiaries, affiliated managers, or independent distributors determine the best price according to their market environment. Prices do not have to be harmonized from country to country.*
- ***Geocentric pricing*** *is more dynamic and proactive. It is based on the consideration of local factors in local markets. These factors are local costs, revenue levels, competition, and local marketing strategies.*

The other strategies used in international pricing are as follows.

6.8 Dumping

Dumping is the sale of goods in foreign markets at a price lower than the domestic price. It sometimes even seeks to capture international markets by applying a price below the cost price (Gultekin, 2005: 10).

In practice, dumping is defined as the sale of goods in foreign markets under production costs. In the country where the domestic market is dumping, producers can get harmed; and dumping is unfair competition in international trade (Çelik, 2009: 228).

Dumping is performed in four ways (Karafakioğlu, 2008: 158):

- ***Sporadic dumping:*** *it is often used to destocks in the domestic market and product prices are lowered considerably.*
- ***Predatory dumping:*** *enter the foreign market at low prices; and this approach's aim is to harm local companies.*
- ***Persistent dumping:*** *low price strategy is constantly used in international markets.*
- ***Reverse dumping:*** *the product is sold for a lower price in the domestic market but it is sold for a higher price in the foreign market.*

6.9 Transfer Pricing

It is about the deals with internal exchanges between buyers and sellers affiliated to the main company. The main purpose of this pricing is to reduce the tax burden (Pehlivan, 2006: 80). Also transfer pricing can be applied to intellectual properties such as research, patents, and royalties.

Conclusion

In order for Turkish companies to achieve sustainable profitable growth targets as a regional and global player, pricing makes it an indispensable part of companies. Among the investments made to improve profitability in firms, the return on investments made in the pricing field is higher than any other field.

Also, the price level of a product is one of the factors that determine the success or failure of a company because it affects profitability.

When we look at the price and price-consumer relations in terms of marketing, it is seen that price is a process that is planned to have a positive effect on the buying behavior of the consumer as price informs the consumer about the value of the product.

Whats's more, price is a strategic tool, and it is the most important determinant of business profitability as companies can change the demand with effective pricing and so it effects the sales.

In international markets, pricing policy can prevent potential new competitors from entering the market. For all these reasons, companies should give due consideration to pricing.

Bibliography

Altıntaş, H., Tombak, F., (2011). Türkiye'de Hisse Senedi Fiyatları ve Makro Ekonomik Değişkenler Arasındaki İlişkinin Ekonometrik Analizi: 1987-2008, Paper presented at EconAnadolu 2011: Anadolu International Conference in Economics II.

Aggarwal, R., (1981). Exchange Rates and Stock Prices: A Study of U.S.Capital Market Under Flaoting Exchange Rates.

Akron Business and Economic Review, 12, ss. 7–12.

Aydeniz, E. Ş. (2009). Makroekonomik Göstergelerin Firmaların Finansal Performans Ölçütleri Üzerindeki Etkisinin Ölçülmesine Yönelik Bir Araştırma: İmkb'ye Kote Gıda Ve İçecek İşletmeleri Üzerine Bir Uygulama. *Marmara Üniversitesi İibf Dergisi, Xxvı/Iı*, 263–277.

Bahmani-Oskooee, M. ve Sohrabian, A., (1992). Stock Prices and The Effective Exchange Rate Of The Dolar. Applied Economics, 24, ss. 459–464.

Bayar, N. (2012). *Aile Ve Tüketici Hizmetleri*. Ankara: Ürün Fiyatlandırma.

Beatty, R., & Ritter, J. (1986). Investment banking, reputation, and underpricing of initial public offerings. *Journal of Financial Economics*, *15*, 213–232.

Benli, O. (2006). *İhracatta Fiyatlandırma Ve Teklif Hazırlama, İhracatı Geliştirme Etüd Merkezi*. Ar-Ge Başkanlığı, Araştırma Dairesi, Ankara: İGEME.

Bruhn, M. (2000). *Marketing, Grundlagen Für Studium Und Praxis* (7. Aufl.). Wiesbaden: Gabler Verlag.

Çelik, K. (2009). *Genel Ekonomi* (1. Baskı). Trabzon: Murathan Yayınevi.

Cemalcılar, İ. (1987). Definition of marketing. *Marketing World, 1*(5), 256–277.

Cemalcılar, İ. (1999). *Pazarlama Kavramlar-Kararlar*. İstanbul: Beta Yayıncılık.

Chow, E.H., Lee W.Y. ve Solt M.S., (1997). The Exchange Rate Risk Exposure of Asset Returns. Journal of Business, 70, ss. 105–123.

Doğru, B., & Recepoğlu, M. (2013). Türkiye'de Hisse Senedi Fiyatları Ve Döviz Kuru Arasında Doğrusal Ve Doğrusal Olmayan Eş Bütünleşme İlişkisi. *Dumlupınar Üniversitesi Sosyal Bilimler Dergisi* Eyi *2013* Özel Sayısı, 20–34

Dongwei, S., & Belton, M. F. (1999). An empirical investigation of underpricing in Chinese Ipos. *Pacific-Basin Finance Journal, 7*, 173–202.

Dow, J., & Gorton, G. (1995). *Stock market efficiency and economic efficiency: Is there a connection?* (Nben Working Paper, No. 5233).

Özmen, E., (2007). Financial Development, Exchange Rate Regimes and the Feldstein-Horioka Puzzle: Evidence from the MENA Region. Applied Economics, 39, p.1133–1138.

Franck, P. & Young, A. (1972). Stock Price Reaction of Multinational Firms to Exchange Re-alignments. Financial Management, vol. 1, 1972, pp. 66–73.

Gültekin, S. (2005). *Dünya Ticaret Örgütü Kapsamında Tarım Ürünleri Ve Türkiye, Yayımlanmamış Doktora Tezi*. Trabzon: Ktü Sosyal Bilimler Enstitüsü.

Huibers, F., Raat, W.K., (1994). The Pricing of Public Sector and Private Sector IPOs: Theory and Evidence. Eburon.

Hirt, G. A. (2004). *Managing investments*. Blacklick: Mcgraw-Hill.

İslamoğlu, H. (2013). *Pazarlama Yönetimi Stratejik Yaklaşım* (6. Baskı). İstanbul: Beta Yayıncılık.

İslamoğlu, H. (2014). *Küresel Pazarlama*. İstanbul: Beta Yayıncılık.

Karafakıoğlu, M. (1974). *Pazarlama Bileşeni Olarak Fiyatın Mamul Ve Mamul Hattı İçin Belirlenmesi Ve Türkiye'deki Uygulama*. İstanbul: Doktora Tezi.

Karafakıoğlu, M. (2008). *Uluslararası Pazarlama Yönetimi* (5. Baskı). İstanbul: Beta Yayıncılık.

Karafakıoğlu, M. (2015). *Uluslararası Pazarlama Yönetimi* (9. Baskı). İstanbul: Beta Yayıncılık.

Kasman, A., (2003). Türkiye"de Reel Döviz Kuru Oynaklığı ve Bunun İhracat Üzerine Etkisi: Sektörel Bir Analiz. Uludağ Üniversitesi İktisadi ve İdari Bilimler Fakültesi Dergisi, 22(2), p.169–186.

Keegan, W., & Green, M. (2013). *Global marketing* (7th ed.). New York: Pearson.

Kim, K., (2003). Dollar Exchange Rate and Stock Price: Evidence from Multivariate Cointegration and Error Correction Model. Review of Financial Economics, 12, p.301–313.

Kirkulak, B and Davis, C., 2005. Underwriter Reputation and Underpricing: Evidence from the Japanese IPO Market. Pacific-Basin Finance Journal 13 (4), p. 451–470.

Korkmaz, S., Eser, Z., Öztürk, A., & Işın, B. (2009). *Pazarlama: Kavramlar, Kararlar, İlkeler*. Ankara: Siyasal Kitabevi.

Kotler, P., & Armstrong, G. (2018). *Principles of marketing, Pearson Higher Education* (17th ed.). Boston: Prentice Hall.

Kotler, P., Armstrong, G., Harris, L., & Piercy, N. (2017). *Principles of marketing* (7th European ed.). Cambridge: Prentice-Hall.

Kotler, P., Armstrong, G., Saunders, J., & Wong, V. (1999). *Principles of marketing* (2nd ed.). Cambridge: Prentice-Hall.

Kotler, P., Armstrong, G., Saunders, J., & Wong, V. (2005). *Principles of marketing* (5th European ed.). Cambridge: Prentice-Hall.

Leigh, L. (1995). Financial Development, Economic Growth and the Effect of Financial Innovation on the Demand for Money in an Open Economy-An Econometric.

Mucuk, İ. (2010). *Pazarlama İlkeleri* (18. Baskı). İstanbul: Türkmen Kitabevi.

Nakip, M., Varinli, İ., & Gülmez, M. (2012). *Güncel Pazarlama Yönetimi*. Ankara: Detay Yayıncılık.

Nieh, C.C. ve Lee, C.F., (2001). Dynamic Relationship Between StockPricesand Exchange Rates for G-7 Countries. The Quarterly Review of Economics and Finance, 41, ss. 477–490.

Oluç, M. (1988). Pricing. *Marketing World, 2*(10), 9–10.

Ozair, A., (2006). Causality Between Stock prices and Exchange Rates: A Case of The United States. Florida Atlantic University, Master of Science Thesis.

Özer, A., Kaya, A., & Özer, N. (2011). Hisse Senedi Fiyatları İle Makroekonomik Değişkenlerin: Etkileşimi. *Dokuz Eylül Üniversitesi İktisadi İdari Bilimler Fakültesi Dergisi, 26*(1), 163–182. Retrieved from http://dergipark.org.tr/deuiibfd/issue/22731/242593

Öztürk, A. (2017). *Hizmet Pazarlaması* (16. Baskı). Bursa: Ekin Basım Yayın Dağıtım.

Pehlivan, O. (2006). *Uluslararası Vergilendirme*. Trabzon: Derya Kitapevi.

Peter, J. P., & Donelly, J. H. (1998). *Marketing management knowledge and skills.* Boston: McGraw Hill.

Phylaktis, K. ve Ravazzolo, F., (2005), "Stock Prices and Exchange Rate Dynamics", Journal of International Money and Finance, 24, ss.1031–1053.

Rock, K. (1994). Why New Issues are Underpriced. Journal of Financial Economics, 15, ss.187–212.

Santomero, A. M. (2002). Bankacılık Düzenlemeleri Banka Müşterilerine Nasıl Yansır? *Bankacılar Dergisi, 43,* 101–109.

Soenen, L. A., ve Hennigar, E. S., (1988), "An Analysis of Exchange Rates and Stock Prices: the U.S. Experience between 1980 and 1986", Akron Business and Economic Review, ss.7–16.

Solnik, B., (1987). Using Financial Prices to Test Exchange Rate Models: A Note. Journal of Finance, 42, ss.141–149.

Stanton, W. (1994). *Fundamentals of marketing* (McGraw Hill series in marketing). Boston: McGraw Hill.

Usta, Ö. (2014). *İşletme Finansı Ve Finansal Yönetim* (6. Baskı). Ankara: Detay Yayıncılık.

Yağcı, İ., & Kılıç, S. (Eds.). (2014). *Uluslararası Pazarlama.* İstanbul: Lisans Yayıncılık.

Yükselen, C. (2016). *Pazarlama İlkeler-Yönetim Örnek Olaylar* (13. Baskı). Ankara: Detay Yayıncılık.

Yükselen, C. (2017). *Pazarlama İlkeler-Yönetim Örnek Olaylar* (14. Baskı). Ankara: Detay Yayıncılık.

Index

List of Figures

List of Tables

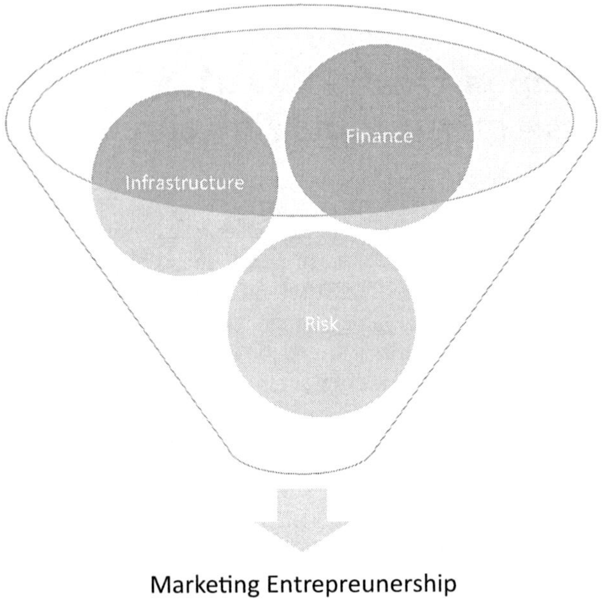

Fig. 1: Marketing Entrepreneurship Funnel

the future are very high. Therefore, any company's financial department will be reluctant to invest in a long-term brand name.

Marketing finance includes the provision and management of the money and credit required to be used in the activities carried out to get the goods into the hands of consumers (Tenekecioğlu & Ersoy, 1999). Marketing that does not have the necessary financial funds will not develop enough in the economy. Economies of countries with a strong financial system are developed, and thus their marketing infrastructure is improved.

In terms of marketing, venture capital is an important source of funding. Because it encourages the emergence of innovative ideas to respond to changing customer demands. However, an important feature of undeveloped capital markets is predominantly reserving tangible assets to allocation of financial funds (Braun, 2003). This situation, which leads to a limited relationship between the entrepreneur and the investor, makes access to capital difficult.

Venture capital is long-term investments made by investors with surplus capital funds for the formation and operation of companies with high development potential. The aim of the venture capital investment is to obtain the profit from

Adnan Kara

Chapter One: Marketing Finance, Infrastructure, and Entrepreneurship

Abstract: This chapter examines the relationship between marketing finance, infrastructure, and entrepreneurship. The aim of the study is to show that countries' financial development improves infrastructure, reduces risks, and increases entrepreneurship. Marketing finance is the provision and management of monetary funds in order to carry out marketing activities. Marketing infrastructure is the existence of physical systems such as logistics, advertising agencies and research companies that carry out marketing activities. Marketing entrepreneurship is the transformation of innovative ideas into economic activities in coordination with marketing process management. In conclusion of the study, the development of the financial system affects the competitiveness. Thus, more marketing investments are made in a more competitive environment.

Keywords: Marketing entrepreneurship, marketing finance, marketing infrastructure, marketing risk

Introduction

Marketing helps raise standards in society and develop distribution channels. In the economic system supported by advanced distribution channels, suitable environments for entrepreneurship are created.

As seen on Fig. 1, marketing entrepreneurship is conclusion of risk, infrastructure, and finance. In high-risk environments, marketing entrepreneurs maximize profit and minimize risk. Sophisticated infrastructure and financial system facilitate this marketing task.

1 Marketing Finance

Marketing mostly focuses on intangible assets such as brand, image, and promotion. Finance, on the other hand, focuses on short-term cash flows. Finance can be expressed as a common branch of economy and business that allows individuals and institutions to invest. Price instability, weakness of financial contracts, inability to protect intangible assets, and inadequate technologic improvements are the characteristics of undeveloped financial systems (Braun, 2003). These factors are indicative of how the development of the financial system may affect marketing. For example, in a politically unstable country, uncertainties about